Tying Headbands or Venus Appearing: New Translations of *k'al*, the Dresden Codex Venus Pages and Classic Period Royal 'Binding' Rituals

Gerardo Aldana y Villalobos

BAR International Series 2239
2011

Published in 2016 by
BAR Publishing, Oxford

BAR International Series 2239

Tying Headbands or Venus Appearing: New Translations of k'al, *the Dresden Codex Venus
Pages and Classic Period Royal 'Binding' Rituals*

ISBN 978 1 4073 0803 6

BAR Publishing is the trading name of British Archaeological Reports (Oxford) Ltd.
British Archaeological Reports was first incorporated in 1974 to publish the BAR
Series, International and British. In 1992 Hadrian Books Ltd became part of the BAR
group. This volume was originally published by Archaeopress in conjunction with
British Archaeological Reports (Oxford) Ltd / Hadrian Books Ltd, the Series principal
publisher, in 2011. This present volume is published by BAR Publishing, 2016.

Printed in England

BAR
PUBLISHING

BAR titles are available from:

BAR Publishing
122 Banbury Rd, Oxford, OX2 7BP, UK
EMAIL   info@barpublishing.com
PHONE   +44 (0)1865 310431
FAX   +44 (0)1865 316916
www.barpublishing.com

Abstract

Epigraphers of the Mayan hieroglyphic writing system have demonstrated that a single verb root lies behind a substantial array of royal rituals. At the same time, astronomically oriented studies have found the same root associated with the events of celestial bodies. Perhaps the best known of the latter is the operative verb within the Dresden Codex Venus Pages. This paper tackles ostensibly minor incongruities within current interpretations of the Venus Pages to reveal a trajectory that resolves the difference between astronomical and epigraphic treatments of the verb in question. In an attempt to ameliorate these inconsistencies, textual data external to the Dresden Codex both temporally and geographically are brought into consideration. The external data reveals an unexpected linguistic and thematic continuity, which further challenges current calendric interpretations of the Venus Pages. Rectifying the calendric inconsistency requires a substantial reinterpretation of the procedure for utilizing the Preface to the Venus Table; in so doing, a new solution to the long enigmatic interval of 9,100 days is proposed. This last move introduces a reconsideration of the Venus Table in its entirety, with a focus on *k'al*, the operative verb throughout the table, such that we gain access to a perspective of ritual time and space that appears to have been held throughout Mesoamerica. This essay appeals to calendrics, iconography, hieroglyphs, and architecture to suggest that *k'al* referred to a ritual 'enclosing' or 'loop-tracing' in space and time.

Table of Contents

List of Figures

List of Tables

Preface

At some level the contextualization of this manuscript must begin with something of a confessional. That is, my own doctoral training occurred at an awkward moment in the decipherment of Mayan hieroglyphic writing. Although it was precisely at the time period during which David Stuart, Stephen Houston, and John Robertson were formulating their Classic Ch'olti'an thesis and I was at the time taking classes from Stuart, their unfolding research could not yet be distilled into actual methodological training. Complicating matters for me is that my doctoral training was based in the history of science even though my overall training was split between archaeology and history. Thus my formal language training was in French and Latin, and I only picked up a scattered familiarity with Yucatec and Ch'orti' Mayan through summer research travel.

The fruits of the latest revolution in Mayan epigraphy thus came about as I was writing my dissertation and then fumbling through my first years as an assistant professor. This is all to say that while I have focused my attention on the astronomical content of the hieroglyphic inscriptions for my research endeavors, my attempts to catch up with the epigraphic wave of developments through individual study and attendance at the Texas Meetings left me feeling as though I was falling steadily behind.

A new opportunity arose, however, with my sabbatical starting in the 2008 – 09 academic year. Dr. Marianne Mithun offered an introductory class on Native American languages during the Fall of 2009 at UCSB, which I eagerly audited. This formal introduction to Native American grammar piqued my interest in what I thought would be a reasonable project for the term. Specifically, I set myself the goal of understanding the different suffixes showing up on an interesting verb root—one found in royal ritual as well as astronomical contexts. In particular, my interest was triggered by a –yi affixed to –wa and –ni in an inscription from Classic period Copan. Since the analysis of CVC root transitive verbs had received substantial study of late, it seemed fertile soil for a focused immersion into Mayan linguistics. While I do feel as though I have made substantial progress on that front, it was actually another aspect of the problem that led to this book.

Not long before my sabbatical, I had taken a new interest in the Dresden Codex Venus Table. One part of its traditional interpretation in particular began to bother me and it seemed directly involved with the reading of the verb root I was studying for Marianne's class: k'al. So it was this complication—a concern with reading k'al and its implications for reading the Venus Table—that set me on the path that turned into this manuscript.

Clearly, then, I owe a great debt to Marianne Mithun for gently guiding me into indigenous language linguistic analysis—though, of course, I absolve her from any and all errors that may nevertheless have made it into the final essay. The epigraphic aspects of this research were greatly aided by the database of hieroglyphs created by Martha Macri and her colleagues at UC Davis, as well as digital images of thousands of hieroglyphic texts provided by Alexandre Tokovinine (years ago at an Advanced Grammar workshop within the Texas Meetings).

I am also grateful for early commentary on my attempts at re-interpreting *k'al* in the Dresden Codex offered by Alfonso Lacadena and Søren Wichmann at the 2008 European Maya Conference in Paris. Once the core of the argument was formulated, it enjoyed a vigorous vetting by Anthony Aveni, Hal Green, and Lloyd Anderson, who contributed to a shifting in emphasis of the overall essay. Two additional scholars greatly aided my confidence in the argument with their own commentary, though with that commentary they requested anonymity.

Ed Barnhart followed with a thorough critique of the first draft of the essay, and then heard me present much of the argument along with Chris Powell, Hal Green (again), and Michael Grofe at the Kalpulli Ce Akatl advanced seminar on Mayan astronomy (hosted by the Chicano Studies Institute at UCSB during the summer of 2009). At the CSULA Mesoamerican Conference, the argument benefited from a receptive audience and a subsequent heavy editing to elaborate on those points that seemed to raise the most questions for a more general audience.

The final form of the manuscript very much benefited further from my sabbatical leave provided by UCSB; a travel grant provided by the UCSB Academic Senate; a teaching release generously granted by the IHC at UCSB; the resources of the CSI and the clear skies and open western horizon of Goleta, California. My appreciation, of course, always goes out as well to Cita, Lulu, and Seri. But this book is dedicated to the teacher I lamentably never had the fortune of meeting in person: Floyd Lounsbury. It is my sincere hope that he would have recognized his influence within my work, and found some value in the results.

INTRODUCTION

According to the contemporary literature, the Dresden Codex Venus Table enjoys a tremendous degree of consensus in interpretation. It also is often invoked as evidence of the cultural and intellectual heights achieved by the literati of ancient Mayan[1] civilization.

"Of the surviving Precolumbian Maya hieroglyphic books, the Dresden Codex… is the one that gives the most information about astronomy, and one of the major astronomical instruments in the Dresden Codex is the Venus table… This table has been studied for more than a century, and it is probably the best known and most cited part of any of the Precolumbian Maya books" (Bricker and Bricker 2007:95).

"The corrected Venus ephemeris places the user within two hours of the true position of Venus in the sky after 301 Venus revolutions (481 years). With such a set of corrections the table could have been used almost indefinitely. Again, achievement of this kind of accuracy is truly extraordinary" (Aveni 2001:189).

"In fact, working from information in the introduction to the main table (page 24), modern scholars are unanimous in associating the specific base date referred to in lines 13 and 14 of the table with 11.0.3.1.0 1 Ahau 13 Mac (June 15, 1227 by the 584,285 conversion constant)" (Paxton 2001:69).

At some level, this should come as no surprise given the concerted attention the manuscript has received over the last century and a half. By all accounts, the only substantial ambiguity still unresolved concerns the purpose of a single number on the first of the Venus pages. Even this has not drawn much attention as, for instance, Eric Thompson readily dismissed it as a copyist's mistake (1972:63). However it is interpreted,

one outstanding number is a small blemish on an otherwise masterful academic reconstruction of the utility of the Dresden Codex Venus Table. Like a Russian doll's outer shell, though, the beauty of this representation hides a subtle yet well-defined crack revealing an interpretive layer beneath it, along with the problem it masks.

Sticking to the Russian doll analogy, this essay begins with an exterior shell of Venus's warrior identity. A careful consideration of the source and justification of Venus as a warrior deity reveals a critical inconsistency in the Venus Table's interpretation, which, as benign as it may seem, concerns a choice between two glosses of the operative verb. The verb in question is the one Eric Thompson numbered 713, and described as the 'il-hand verb.' (See Figure 1) We will find in the first chapter that current differences in reading this term derive from a methodological divide giving preference to one form of data over another—sub-fields of the discipline. Through an examination of this conflict we are led to the recognition of a more significant incoherence generated by *either* gloss. For any hope of resolution, we are forced to look outside the manuscript itself for further data.

Unfortunately, the Dresden Codex is without specific provenance—it is a single data point unmoored to archaeological context or historical environment. In order to address the otherwise isolated problem of Venus's identity crisis, then, we turn to an untapped intellectual context for the Venus Table. In the second chapter (the third Doll from the center), we turn to a unique hieroglyphic record at Copan. The inscriptions on the walls of Structure 10L-11 provide a clear argument for conceptual continuity between the astronomical traditions of the Late Classic at Copan and the middle Postclassic traditions of the Dresden Codex. In both cases, Venus events are described using T713, deciphered as **K'AL** in the 1990s, but still without clear consistent gloss. This continuity, however, reveals an opportunity to re-evaluate the traditional calendric interpretations (post 1930) of Page 24, the appropriately named Preface to the Venus Table. Exploring these calendric issues provides a more

[1] The convention in Maya Studies is to use "Mayan" only for languages, and "Maya" for everything else. John Justeson and David Tavarez (2007) recently provided a compelling argument for following suit with European (and derivative) adjectives, which I accept here.

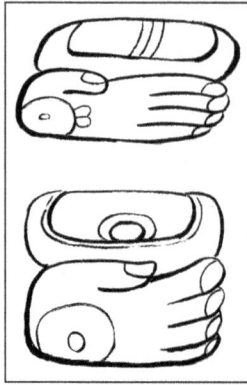

Figure 1: T713, Thompson's '*il*-hand verb,'
logographic K'AL

robust alternative reading of this page as well as a solution to the long outstanding problem of the purpose of the interval 1.5.5.0.

By this point in the essay, the traditional reading of the Dresden Codex Venus Table becomes non-trivially de-stabilized. At the same time, we confront a new alternative—one with a number of compelling qualities, but also one that would be asked to take on a Herculean task of replacing the 'standard model.' On the other hand, the alternative proposed here gains credibility in its productivity beyond the Dresden Codex. The next chapter (second doll from the center) turns to other astronomical records also dependent on T713 in order to work toward a solution for the troublesome verb. Comparing solar and lunar records from the Classic period inscriptions with the use of T713 in the Venus Table demonstrates an interpretive shift in the gloss. There we find that *k'al* events in astronomical contexts refer to the completion of sub-periods. While we might be tempted to see this as an abstraction of 'tying' or 'wrapping,' this observation still leaves us one step short of resolution to the new found anomalies in the Dresden Codex Venus Table.

The final chapter, Doll 1, turns to iconography to suggest an overall coherence to all instances of T713 in hieroglyphic contexts. I suggest at end that this coherence is evidenced by a comparison of the Féjérvary-Mayer and Madrid "cosmograms" to the text of the Dresden Codex Venus Table. In this specific case, I take *k'al* as the 'tracing out of a closed loop' to conclude that the Féjérvary-Mayer and Madrid images do with illustrations what the Dresden does with text. The process terminates, therefore, with a consideration of core conceptual and methodological assumptions about Mayan time and astronomy. Re-translating this core produces a new reading—not only of the Dresden Codex Venus Table, but of time and ritual space in ancient Mesoamerica.

Chapter 1:
READING METHODS, THE FOURTH DOLL

4.3 ASTRONOMICAL 'APPEARANCE'

The astronomical interpretation of the operative verb in the Dresden Codex Venus pages goes all the way back to its first consideration at the end of the nineteenth century. The German librarian and philologist Ernst Förstemann was the first in modern times to recognize that the four columns on the left hand sides of pages 46 through 50 tracked intervals within the 260-day count that summed to 584 (1891:117-122). (See Figures 2 & 3) The latter number, he noted, was very close to the synodic period of Venus. (See Figure 4) While presenting data from his own observations from 1882 through 1884 to justify the periods of 8 and 90 as reasonable accounts for Venus's invisibility (inferior and superior conjunction respectively (See Figure 5)), Förstemann acknowledged a lack of comprehension regarding the asymmetry between the other two intervals:

> "As to the evening star period of 250, and the morning star period of 236 days, I confess that my astronomical knowledge is too small for me to be able to explain this inequality; in reality it is usual to give these two periods, which are not exactly equal, 243 days each" (Förstemann 1891:121).

A few years later, Förstemann advanced his understanding of Page 24 to now recognize in it a table of multiples of Venus periods. Therein he found thirteen multiples of 2,920 (= 5 x 584), three multiples of 37,960 (= 13 x 2,920), and four anomalous intervals that were nevertheless multiples of 260 (1891:82-82; 1894). Integrating his new calendric insights into Paul Schellhas's deity classification system, Förstemann provided an overall interpretation of Page 24 based almost exclusively on numerical patterns:

> "we find that the Indian writer desires to say this:
>
> I am here treating especially the periods consisting of five successive Venus years, bringing them into harmony with the solar year and the tonalamatl. I am

at the same time considering a second important period, that in which the two heavenly bodies of the second class, the moon and Mercury, come together in their orbits, a period made up of four unequal parts. Just in the same way is each individual Venus year divided into four unequal parts, which appertain to the east, north, west, and south and are ruled by certain deities, which I can mention only in part, owing to lack of space. Lastly, I would add that each of the five Venus years of a period is dominated as a whole by a deity, and the signs of these I give here" (1894:443).

Thus, aside from the appeal to a role for Mercury, Förstemann elucidated most of what is still understood of Venus's appearances throughout Pages 24 and 46 through 50 of the Dresden Codex.

Yet there was still work to be done, and it was Eduard Seler who advanced the collective understanding one substantial step further by comparing Förstemann's work with that on several of the known "Mexican codices." Seler's eye for iconography was put to tremendous use in the comparison of the Dresden Codex Venus pages to the imagery and calendric patterns within the Codices Telleriano-Remensis, Aubin, Borgia, and the Anales de Cuauhtitlan. These associations led him to depart from Förstemann's view that the Venus Table illustrations depicted the repeated battles between the Sun and Venus (Förstemann 1891:122; Seler 1904:382-391). Instead, Seler saw a direct correspondence between the imagery of the Borgia Codex and the description of Quetzalcoatl's apotheosis as Venus in the Anales de Cuauhtitlan. (See Figure 6)

The many specific connections between this passage and the imagery and text of the Venus pages have since formed the core of scholarly views of Venus in the Dresden Codex (Aveni 2001:184-196; Bricker and Bricker 2007:106-109; Paxton 2001:64-81; Seler 1904; Thompson 1972:62-71). Key here are the recognitions that each period of Venus's (in)visibility is associated

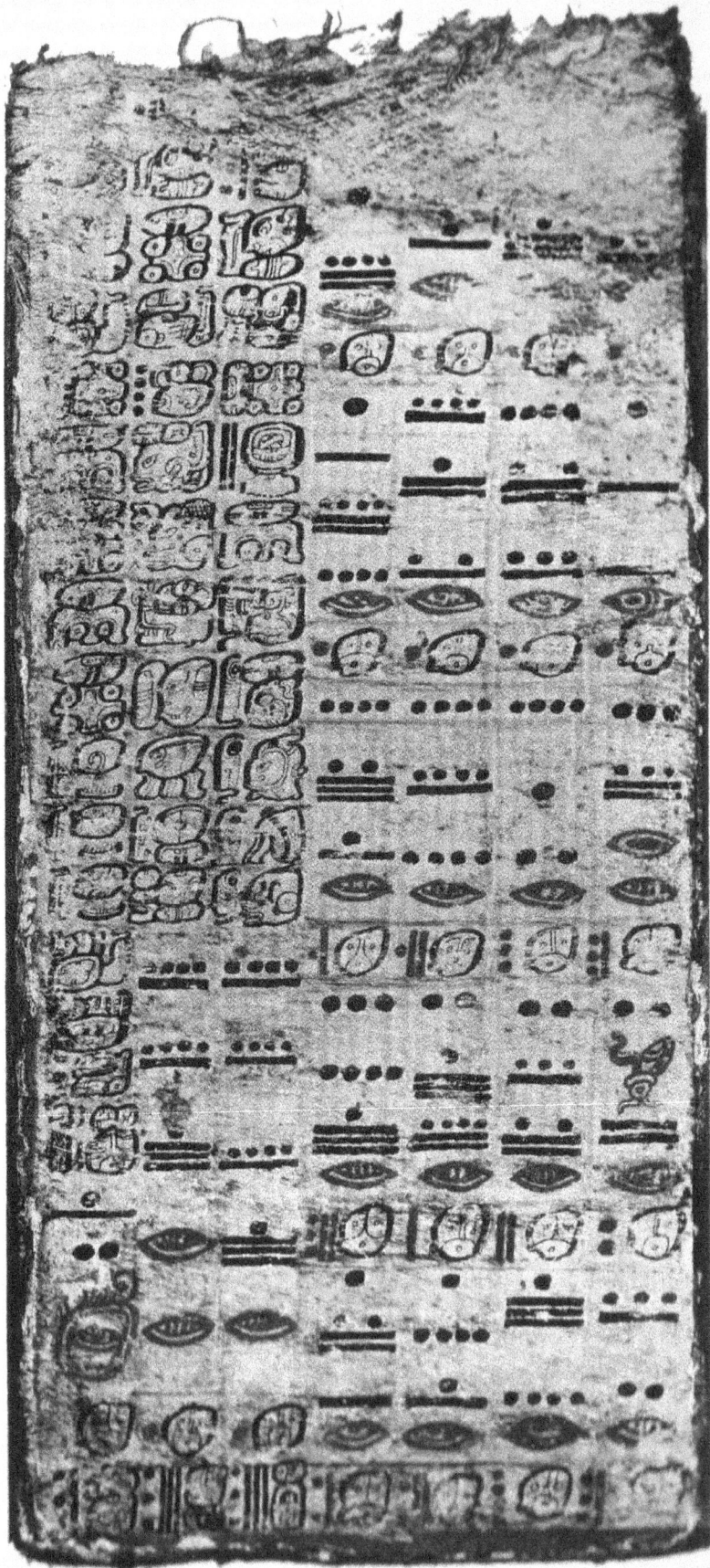

Figure 2a: Page 24 of the Dresden Codex
(image from the Förstemann facsimile obtained from www.famsi.org)

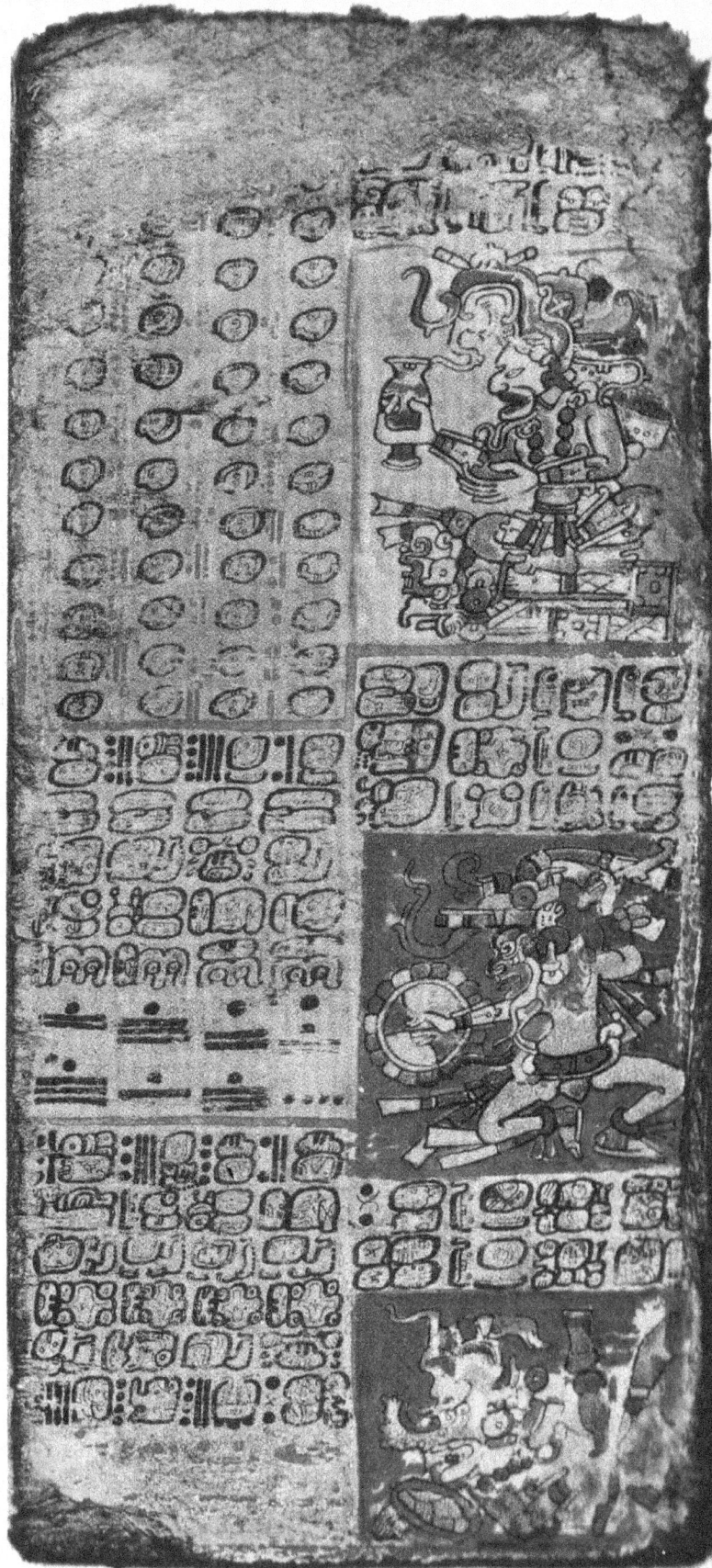

Figure 2b: Page 46 of the Dresden Codex
(image from the Förstemann facsimile obtained from www.famsi.org)

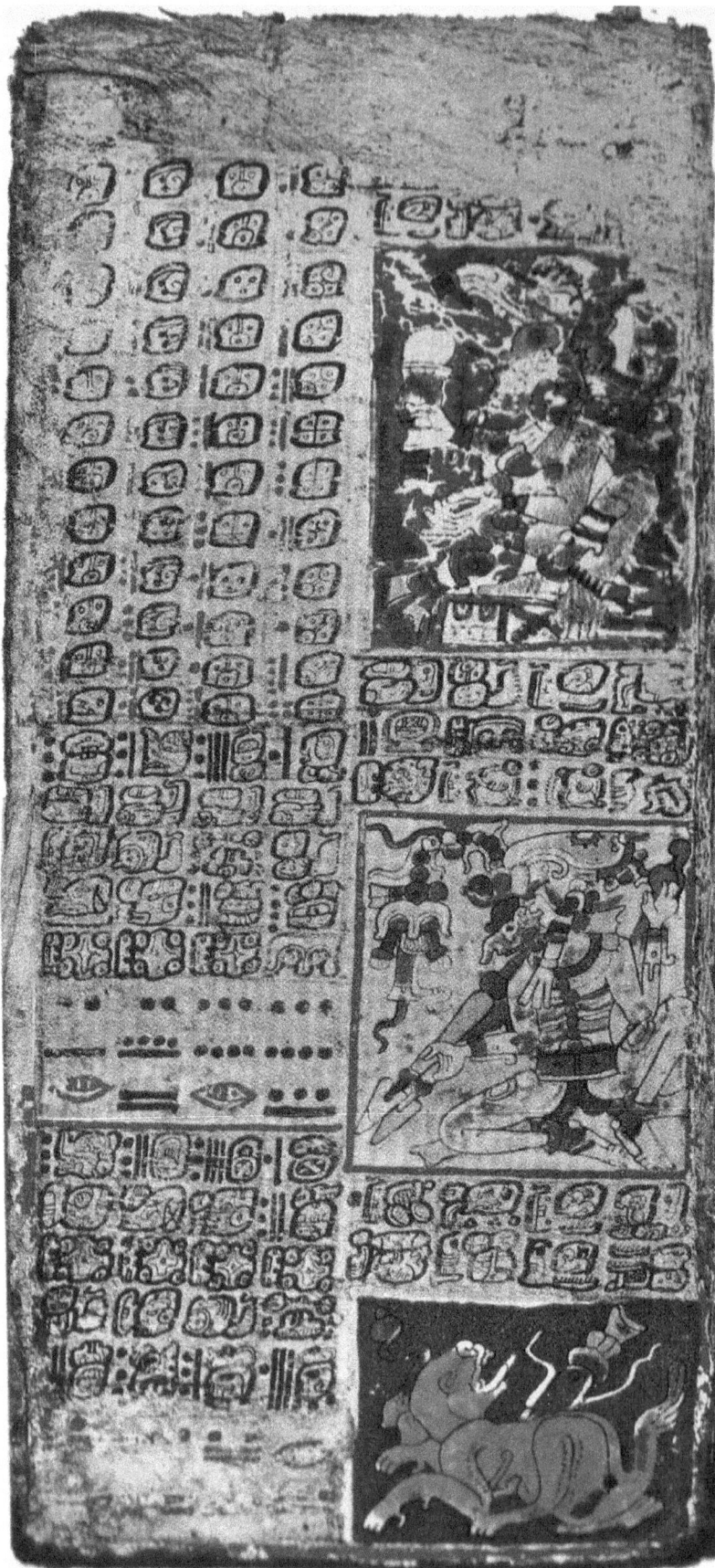

Figure 2c: Page 47 of the Dresden Codex
(image from the Förstemann facsimile obtained from www.famsi.org)

Figure 2d: Page 48 of the Dresden Codex
(image from the Förstemann facsimile obtained from www.famsi.org)

Figure 2e: Page 49 of the Dresden Codex
(image from the Förstemann facsimile obtained from www.famsi.org)

Figure 2f: Page 50 of the Dresden Codex
(image from the Förstemann facsimile obtained from www.famsi.org)

PAGE 24						
A1	B1	C1	1			
A2	B2	8 Kumk'u	1	15	10	5
A3	CHAK EK'	C3	1	16	10	5
			14	6	16	8
			0	0	0	0
			(= 151,840 = 4x37,960)	(= 113,880 = 3x37,960)	(= 75,920 = 2x37,960)	(= 37,960 = 13x2,920)
east	k'ahlaj	Y_1	1 Ajaw	1 Ajaw	1 Ajaw	1 Ajaw
CHAK EK'	X_2	CHAK EK'	1			
CHAK EK'	X_3	Y_2	5	9	4	1
CHAK EK'	X_4	CHAK EK'	14	11	12	5
			4	7	8	5
			0	0	0	0
			(= 185,120)	(= 68,900)	(= 33,280)	(= 9,100)
CHAK EK'	X_5	Z_1	1 Ajaw	1 Ajaw	1 Ajaw	1 Ajaw
CHAK EK'	X_1	Z_2	4	4	4	3
u muuk	B10	Z_3	17	9	1	13
u muuk	B11	Z_4	6	4	2	0
			0	0	0	0
			(= 12x2,920)	(= 11x2,920)	(= 10x2,920)	(= 9x2,920)
u muuk	B12	Z_5	6 Ajaw	11 Ajaw	3 Ajaw	8 Ajaw
A13			3	2	2	2
A14	9	9	4	16	8	0
A15	9	9	16	14	12	10
	16	9	0	0	0	0
	0	16	(= 8x2,920)	(= 7x2,920)	(= 6x2,920)	(= 5x2,920)
6	0	0	13 Ajaw	5 Ajaw	10 Ajaw	2 Ajaw
2			1	1		
(0)			12	4	16	8
			5	6	4	2
			0	0	0	0
4 Ajaw	1 Ajaw	1 Ajaw	(= 4x2,920)	(= 3x2,920)	(= 2x2,920)	(= 1x2,920 = 5x584)
8 Kumk'u	18 K'ayab	18 Wo	7 Ajaw	12 Ajaw	4 Ajaw	9 Ajaw

Figure 3a: translation of Page 24 of the Dresden Codex

PAGE 46							
3 Kib	2 Kimi	5 Kib	13 K'an	L1	M1	N1	O1
11 Kib	10 Kimi	13 Kib	8 K'an	L2	M2	N2	O2
6 Kib	5 Kimi	8 Kib	3 K'an	L3	M3	N3	O3
1 Kib	13 Kimi	3 Kib	11 K'an	Illustration of X_5			
9 Kib	8 Kimi	11 Kib	6 K'an				
4 Kib	3 Kimi	6 Kib	1 K'an				
12 Kib	11 Kimi	1 Kib	9 K'an				
7 Kib	6 Kimi	9 Kib	4 K'an				
2 Kib	1 Kimi	4 Kib	12 K'an				
10 Kib	9 Kimi	12 Kib	7 K'an				
5 Kib	4 Kimi	7 Kib	2 K'an				
13 Kib	12 Kimi	2 Kib	10 K'an				
8 Kib	7 Kimi	10 Kib	5 K'an	k'alaj	East	N13	O13
4 Yaxk'in	14 Sak	19 Tsek	7 Xul	Y_1	Chak Ek'	u muuk	O14
k'al	k'al	k'al	k'al	Z_1	u hul	N15	O15
North	West	South	East	Illustration of Y_1			
U_1	V_1	W_1	X_1				
Chak Ek'	Chak Ek'	Chak Ek'	Chak Ek'				
11 / 16 / (=236)	16 / 6 / (=326)	1 / 10 / 16 / (=576)	1 / 11 / 4 / (=584)				
9 Sak	19 Muwan	4 Yax	12 Yax	L21	u muuk	N21	O21
X_5	U_1	V_1	W_1	L22	u muuk	N22	O22
tse?-ya-ni	tse?-ya-ni	tse?-ya-ni	tse?-ya-ni				
Chak Ek'	Chak Ek'	Chak Ek'	Chak Ek'	Illustration of Z_1			
East	North	West	South				
19 K'ayab	4 Sots'	14 Pax	2 K'ayab				
11 / 16 / (=236)	4 / 10 / (=90)	12 / 10 / (=250)	0 / 8 / (=8)				

Figure 3b: translation of Page 46 of the Dresden Codex

PAGE 47							
2 Ajaw	1 Ok	4 Ajaw	12 Lamat	T1	U1	V1	W1
10 Ajaw	9 Ok	12 Ajaw	7 Lamat	T2	U2	V2	W2
5 Ajaw	4 Ok	7 Ajaw	2 Lamat	u muuk	U3	V3	W3
13 Ajaw	12 Ok	2 Ajaw	10 Lamat				
8 Ajaw	7 Ok	10 Ajaw	5 Lamat				
3 Ajaw	2 Ok	5 Ajaw	13 Lamat				
11 Ajaw	10 Ok	13 Ajaw	8 Lamat				
6 Ajaw	5 Ok	8 Ajaw	3 Lamat	Illustration of X_1			
1 Ajaw	13 Ok	3 Ajaw	11 Lamat				
9 Ajaw	8 Ok	11 Ajaw	6 Lamat				
4 Ajaw	3 Ok	6 Ajaw	1 Lamat				
12 Ajaw	11 Ok	1 Ajaw	9 Lamat				
7 Ajaw	6 Ok	9 Ajaw	4 Lamat	k'ahlaj	East	u muuk	W13
3 Kumk'u	8 Sots'	18 Pax	6 K'ayab	Y_2	Chak Ek'	V14	W14
k'ahlaj	k'ahlaj	k'ahlaj	k'ahlaj	Z_2	u hul	V15	W15
North	West	South	East				
U_2	V_2	W_2	X_2				
Chak Ek'	Chak Ek'	Chak Ek'	Ek'				
2	2	3	3				
5	9	4	4	Illustration of Y_2			
0	10	0	8				
(=820)	(=910)	(=1160)	(= 1168 = 2 x 584)				
3 Sots'	13 Mol	18 Wo	6 Sip				
X_1	U_2	V_2	W_2	T21	U21	u muuk	W21
Chak Ek'	Chak Ek'	Chak Ek'	Chak Ek'	T22	U22	u muuk	W22
East	North	West	South				
13 Yax	3 Muwan	8 Ch'en	16 Ch'en	Illustration of Z_2			
11	4	12	0				
16	10	10	8				
(=236)	(=90)	(=250)	(=8)				

Figure 3c: translation of Page 47 of the Dresden Codex

PAGE 48							
1 K'an	13 Ix	3 K'an	11 Eb	AB1	AC1	AD1	AE1
9 K'an	8 Ix	11 K'an	6 Eb	AB2	AC2	AD2	AE2
4 K'an	3 Ix	6 K'an	1 Eb	AB3	AC3	u muuk	AE3
12 K'an	11 Ix	1 K'an	9 Eb				
7 K'an	6 Ix	9 K'an	4 Eb				
2 K'an	1 Ix	4 K'an	12 Eb				
10 K'an	9 Ix	12 K'an	7 Eb				
5 K'an	4 Ix	7 K'an	2 Eb	Illustration of X_2			
13 K'an	12 Ix	2 K'an	10 Eb				
8 K'an	7 Ix	10 K'an	5 Eb				
3 K'an	2 Ix	5 K'an	13 Eb				
11 K'an	10 Ix	13 K'an	8 Eb				
6 K'an	5 Ix	8 K'an	3 Eb	k'ahlaj	East	u muuk	AE13
17 Yax	7 Muwan	12 Ch'en	0 Yax	Y_3	Chak Ek'	AD14	AE14
k'ahlaj	k'ahlaj	k'ahlaj	k'ahlaj	Z_3	u hul	u muuk	AE15
North	West	South	East				
U_3	V_3	W_3	X_3				
Chak Ek'	Chak Ek'	Chak Ek'	Chak Ek'				
3	4	4	4				
16	2	15	15	Illustration of Y_3			
4	14	4	12				
(=1404)	(=1494)	(=1744)	(= 1752 = 3 x 584)				
2 Muwan	7 Pohp	17 Mak	5 K'ank'in				
tse?-ya-ni	tse?-ya-ni	tse?-ya-ni	tse?-ya-ni	AB21	AC21	AD21	u muuk
X_2	U_3	V_3	W_3	u muuk	AC22	AD22	AE22
East	North	West	South				
7 Sip	17 Yaxk'in	2 Wo	10 Wo				
11	4	12	0				
16	10	10	8	Illustration of Z_3			
(=236)	(=90)	(=250)	(=8)				

Figure 3d: translation of Page 48 of the Dresden Codex

PAGE 49							
13 Lamat	12 Etz'nab	2 Lamat	10 Kib	AJ1	AK1	AL1	AM1
8 Lamat	7 Etz'nab	10 Lamat	5 Kib	u muuk	AK2	AL2	AM2
3 Lamat	2 Etz'nab	5 Lamat	13 Kib	AJ3	AK3	AL3	AM3
11 Lamat	10 Etz'nab	13 Lamat	8 Kib	Illustration of X_3			
6 Lamat	5 Etz'nab	8 Lamat	3 Kib				
1 Lamat	13 Etz'nab	3 Lamat	11 Kib				
9 Lamat	8 Etz'nab	11 Lamat	6 Kib				
4 Lamat	3 Etz'nab	6 Lamat	1 Kib				
12 Lamat	11 Etz'nab	1 Lamat	9 Kib				
7 Lamat	6 Etz'nab	9 Lamat	4 Kib				
2 Lamat	1 Etz'nab	4 Lamat	12 Kib				
10 Lamat	9 Etz'nab	12 Lamat	7 Kib				
5 Lamat	4 Etz'nab	7 Lamat	2 Kib	k'ahlaj	East	u muuk	AM13
11 Sip	1 Mol	6 Wo	14 Wo	Y_4	Chak Ek'	u muuk	AM14
k'ahlaj	k'ahlaj	k'ahlaj	k'ahlaj	Z_4	u hul	u muuk	AM15
North	West	South	East	Illustration of Y_4			
U_4	V_4	W_4	X_4				
Chak Ek'	Chak Ek'	Chak Ek'	Chak Ek'				
5 9 8 (= 1988)	5 13 18 (= 2078)	6 8 4 (= 2328)	6 8 16 (= 2336 = 4 x 584)				
16 Yaxk'in	6 Keh	11 Xul	19 Xul				
tse?-ya-ni	tse?-ya-ni	tse?-ya-ni	tse?-ya-ni	AJ21	AK21	u muuk	AM21
X_3	U_4	V_4	W_4	AJ22	AK22	u muuk	AM22
Chak Ek'	Chak Ek'	Chak Ek'	Chak Ek'				
East	North	West	South				
6 K'ank'in	16 Kumk'u	1 Mak	9 Mak	Illustration of Z_4			
11 16 (=236)	4 10 (=90)	12 10 (=250)	0 8 (=8)				

Figure 3e: translation of Page 49 of the Dresden Codex

PAGE 50							
12 Eb	11 Ik'	1 Eb	9 Ajaw	AR1	Chak Ek'	u muuk	AU1
7 Eb	6 Ik'	9 Eb	4 Ajaw	AR2	AS2	AT2	AU2
2 Eb	1 Ik'	4 Eb	12 Ajaw	AR3	AS3	u muuk	AU3
10 Eb	9 Ik'	12 Eb	7 Ajaw				
5 Eb	4 Ik'	7 Eb	2 Ajaw				
13 Eb	12 Ik'	2 Eb	10 Ajaw				
8 Eb	7 Ik'	10 Eb	5 Ajaw		Illustration of X_4 (with Z_3)		
3 Eb	2 Ik'	5 Eb	13 Ajaw				
11 Eb	10 Ik'	13 Eb	8 Ajaw				
6 Eb	5 Ik'	8 Eb	3 Ajaw				
1 Eb	13 Ik'	3 Eb	11 Ajaw				
9 Eb	8 Ik'	11 Eb	6 Ajaw				
4 Eb	3 Ik'	6 Eb	1 Ajaw	k'ahlaj	East	u muuk	AU13
10 K'ank'in	0 Wayeb	5 Mak	13 Mak	Y_5	Chak Ek'	u muuk	AU14
k'ahlaj	k'ahlaj	k'ahlaj	k'al	Z_5	u hul	u muuk	AU15
North	West	South	East				
U_5	V_5	W_5	X_5				
Chak Ek'	Chak Ek'	Chak Ek'	Chak Ek'				
7 2 12 (= 2572)	7 7 2 (= 2662)	8 1 12 (= 2912)	8 2 0 (= 2920 = 5 x 584)		Illustration of Y_5		
15 Kumk'u	0 Tsek	10 K'ayab	18 K'ayab				
tse?-ya	tse?-ya-ni	tse?-ya-ni	tse?-ya-ni	AR21	u muuk	AT21	u muuk
X_4	U_5	V_5	W_5	AR22	u muuk	AT22	AU22
Chak Ek'	Chak Ek'	Chak Ek'	Chak Ek'				
East	North	West	South				
0 Yaxk'in	10 Sak	15 Tsek	3 Xul		Illustration of Z_5		
11 16 (=236)	4 10 (=90)	12 10 (=250)	0 8 (=8)				

Figure 3f: translation of Page 50 of the Dresden Codex

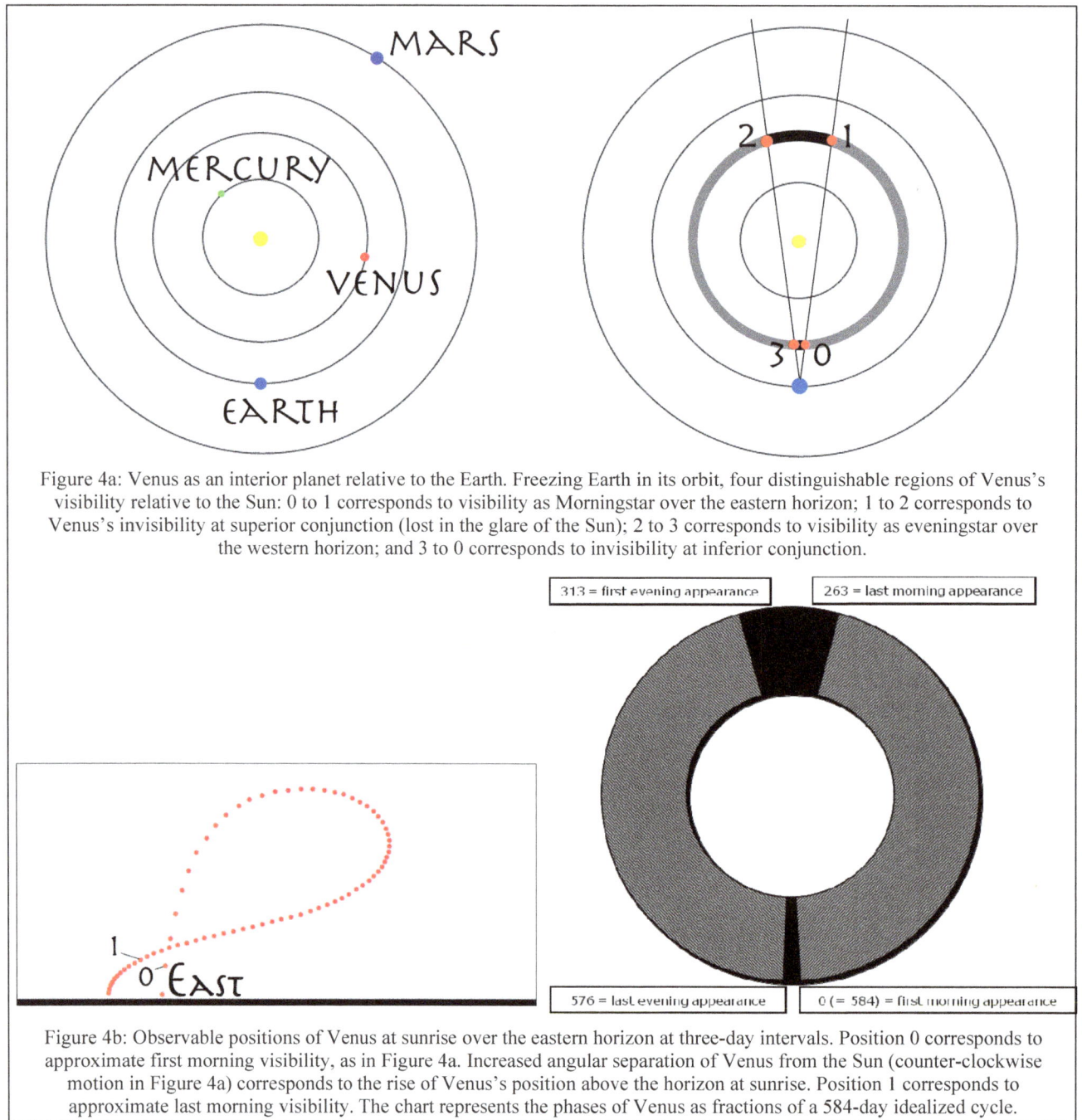

Figure 4a: Venus as an interior planet relative to the Earth. Freezing Earth in its orbit, four distinguishable regions of Venus's visibility relative to the Sun: 0 to 1 corresponds to visibility as Morningstar over the eastern horizon; 1 to 2 corresponds to Venus's invisibility at superior conjunction (lost in the glare of the Sun); 2 to 3 corresponds to visibility as eveningstar over the western horizon; and 3 to 0 corresponds to invisibility at inferior conjunction.

Figure 4b: Observable positions of Venus at sunrise over the eastern horizon at three-day intervals. Position 0 corresponds to approximate first morning visibility, as in Figure 4a. Increased angular separation of Venus from the Sun (counter-clockwise motion in Figure 4a) corresponds to the rise of Venus's position above the horizon at sunrise. Position 1 corresponds to approximate last morning visibility. The chart represents the phases of Venus as fractions of a 584-day idealized cycle.

Figure 4: Venus's synodic period

with a cosmic region.[2] Also, the East appears to be the most important region since it is the cosmic region of the fourth column on the left-hand-side and both the text and images of the right-hand-side elaborate on this eastern event. (See Figure 2 and 3)

Seler, however, was more conservative than those coming after him in his interpretation of these similarities. He wrote that for the Dresden Codex:

"The form armed with the spear thrower and bundle of spears *is not* the deity of the morning star repeated five times, as in the representations of the manuscripts of the Borgian codex group... but five different figures... The figures struck with the spear, on the other hand, are clearly the same as in the representations of the Borgian codex group, at least on the first three pages" (Seler 1904:376, emphasis added).

Because the relationship between Venus and the deities depicted will become a critical issue in this essay, it is worth noting that Seler would only go so far explicitly as to identify these deities as "the regents of the five consecutive Venus periods" (1904:387). Without specifying

---

[2] I refer to the North, South, East, and West as cosmological regions rather than as cardinal directions following the linguistic work of John Watanabe (1983). Specifically, each region captures the movement of the Sun along the horizons over the course of a year along with the Sun's left hand and right hand sides during its daily travel.

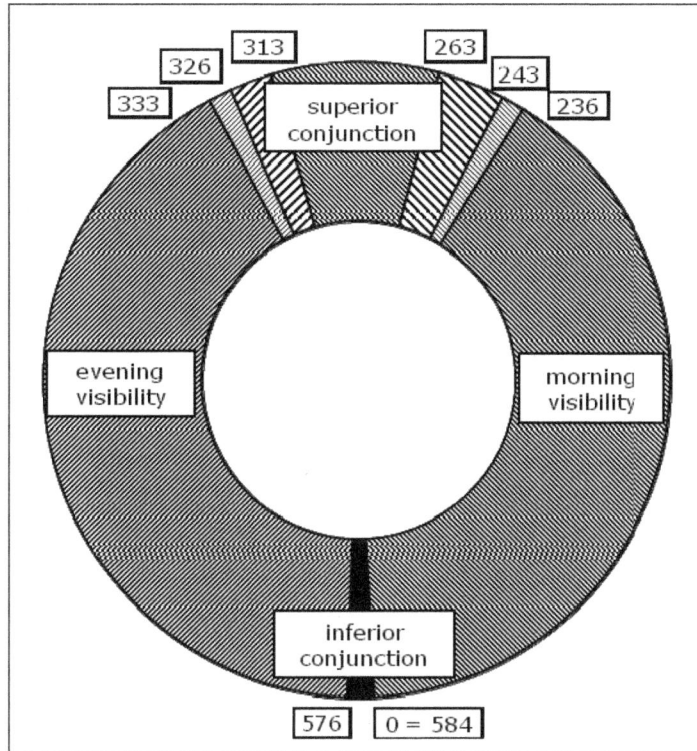

Figure 5: Graph of Venus visibility, including Förstemann's observed periods, Dresden Codex canonical periods, and modern accepted average periods

further what he meant by a "regent," Seler did make it clear that whereas the various figures were "divinities," only the image on page 47 was an actual representation of a/the Venus deity (in morning star form) (1904:388).

Almost seventy years later, Eric Thompson's extensive treatment of the calendrics within the Dresden Codex sought to advance Seler's iconographic inferences through hieroglyphic textual support. By inferring the meaning of individual hieroglyphs rather than linguistically analyzing them (Thompson 1978:289-296; see also Coe 1992:140-142), Thompson suggested numerous "readings" for textual passages throughout the Dresden Codex. Referring to T713, for example, Thompson wrote: "The *il*-hand of line 15 should have some meaning such as appears, is visible, or influences. The clause would then read 'God X appears? in the East [with?] great Venus'" (1972:65). Although most of his readings did not survive the decipherment methodology revolution that followed him, they did provide Thompson the opportunity to address the Venus pages with a larger toolkit. In particular, Thompson's readings changed his interpretation of the spearthrower-holding figures relative to Seler's (1972:65). He argued that these were not 'regents' for Venus periods; they were representations of Venus itself (1972:67).

"On the right of each page of the Venus revolutions are three pictures. ... In the middle... manifestations of the Venus god(s) at heliacal rising after inferior conjunction with spears and spearthrower menace the victim who is shown with dart-pierced body in the bottom ... set of pictures" (1972:67).

Thus Thompson over-rode Seler's more conservative interpretation to suggest that Venus had multiple identities, and each of these was depicted as the spearthrower figure on the right-hand-side of each of these pages.

Archaeoastronomers taking over the subject after Thompson have come to similar if not identical conclusions (Aveni 2001:194; Bricker and Bricker 2007:109; Paxton 2001:80).[3] Certainly, this is due at least in part to the recognition that the calendric structure along with the elements of the hieroglyphic text make it intuitive to follow Thompson's logic. The astronomical pattern strongly implies an 'appears' reading for T713. On the other hand, this does not preclude metaphoric representation, which may be why Anthony Aveni provides *both* the astronomically and the epigraphically weighted glosses to the operative verb in his 2001 revision of *Skywatchers*.

In his treatment of the Venus pages, Aveni provides an illustration giving the "reading" of the text in operation. Here, he goes beyond the text translated by Thompson to include the lower section of text, reading the whole as "On 7 Kan in the East reappears Venus from the South having been absent 8 days" (Aveni 2001:194). However, in the same consideration, Aveni provides a translation of the upper text, following that of Linda Schele and Nikolai Grube (1997). In this case, Aveni gives the first part of the text as: "tied to the east is Kaktonal Great Star,"

---

[3] Paxton writes: "... these dates are associated in lines 15 – 19 with a verb that evidently means 'appear' (or something similar)... (2001:80).

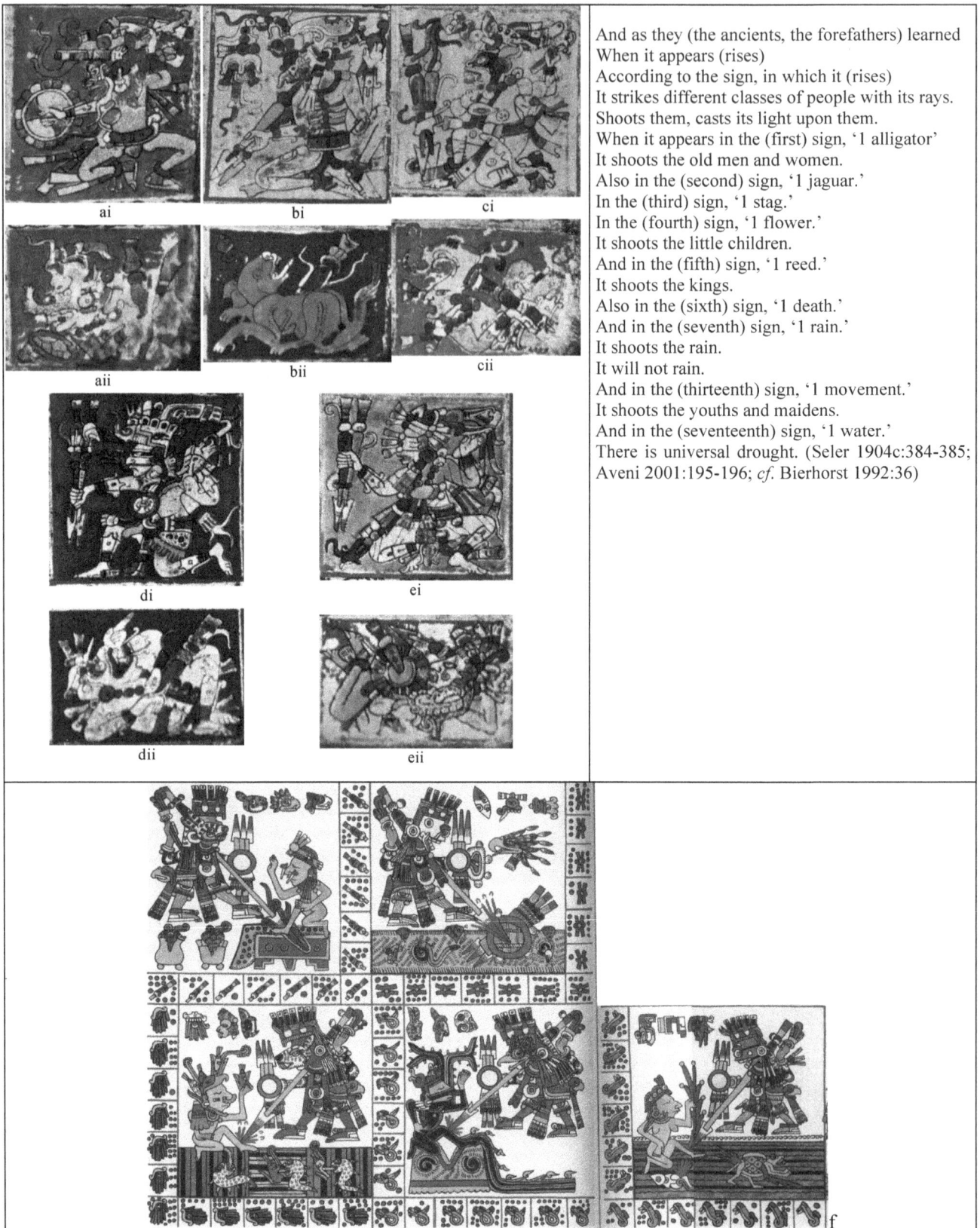

And as they (the ancients, the forefathers) learned
When it appears (rises)
According to the sign, in which it (rises)
It strikes different classes of people with its rays.
Shoots them, casts its light upon them.
When it appears in the (first) sign, '1 alligator'
It shoots the old men and women.
Also in the (second) sign, '1 jaguar.'
In the (third) sign, '1 stag.'
In the (fourth) sign, '1 flower.'
It shoots the little children.
And in the (fifth) sign, '1 reed.'
It shoots the kings.
Also in the (sixth) sign, '1 death.'
And in the (seventh) sign, '1 rain.'
It shoots the rain.
It will not rain.
And in the (thirteenth) sign, '1 movement.'
It shoots the youths and maidens.
And in the (seventeenth) sign, '1 water.'
There is universal drought. (Seler 1904c:384-385;
Aveni 2001:195-196; *cf.* Bierhorst 1992:36)

Figure 6: Summary of Seler's Venus connections across codex representations. ai) – eii) give the warrior figures
and victims in the Venus Pages of the Dresden Codex (images from the Förstemann facsimile obtained from
www.famsi.org); f) warriors and victims from the Venus Pages of the Borgia Codex (by permission from
Dover Publications, Inc.); quote from the Anales de Cuauhtitlan contains Seler's parenthetic count,
which refers to a progression through the 260-day count "signs" by thirteen-day intervals

(2001:193). He has thus captured both readings in the literature: 'Venus appearing' and 'Venus tied,' though apparently without considering them to be in conflict.

4.2 THE HANDS THAT BIND

The other side of this story comes from the substantial hieroglyphic evidence independent of the Venus pages (or anything astronomically related) that supports the reading of a 'tying' or 'binding' of Venus. Thompson's glyph 713, the verb root that controls the recurrent phrase in the Venus pages, occurs frequently within the corpus of Mayan hieroglyphic inscriptions. (Compare Figures 1 and 7) This root, however, has not been deciphered for long.

In 1983, in one of its first extensive treatments, Linda Schele and Jeffrey Miller suggested two semantic values of T713 based on its contexts. They followed George Taack who suggested that the primary element of the glyph was the back of the hand, which then might have held the value of *pach*, or in Cholan and Tzeltalan languages *pat*, meaning both 'the back or end of something' and 'to form/make something' (1983:36). The latter interpretation allowed them to change the reading according to the variable element "held" in the glyphic hand. (See Figure 7)

> "As the main sign in Glyph C of the Lunar Series and as a period-ending glyph for various parts of the katun, T713 appears to have meant 'the end' of the particular cycle as marked by the glyph appearing over (or in) the hand. In accession phrases, it appears to have been read as the verb 'to make.' Paraphrased, T713 would read '(he) was made...' with the glyph for the title assumed placed over (or into) the hand" (1983:36).

Schele and Miller took a similar approach to the case in the Dresden Codex Venus pages, here recognizing it as holding a 'mirror.' They combined an argument for the mirror as *nen* with an interpretation of the role it played to suggest *nentah* 'to shine' (1983:19). This reading fell in line with contemporary astronomical interpretations of the text: 'shining' versus 'appearing.' Yet Schele expressed clear reservations, reflecting a concern with the specific semantic value and not just general interpretation:

> "The primary meaning of the *nen* compound on the Venus pages is perhaps 'shine,' but since Venus is invisible in two of its four phases, the glyph is more likely to mean 'succeeds in office,' referring to the successive initiation of each of the four phases" (1983:20).

Schele's assessment here presaged the eventual decipherment of T713, not through its intuitive connection in the Dresden Codex, but through its tendency toward more heavily weighting a linguistic coherence. Here, she turned to the verb's linguistic relationship to a number of phrases followed by a reflexive clause, *tu b'aah*, 'on him/herself' recognized by Barbara MacLeod (Schele 1999:36). (See Figure 8) MacLeod's work also appealed to the frequent instances of the verb on ceramic drinking vessels within the "Primary Standard Sequence," which led her to suggest a reading of 'to raise' or 'to present' (Stuart 1995:107). Yet

Figure 7: T713 in various compositions. Drawings by the author after Schele (1999:36-38) and Stuart (2006:65-68)

these readings also were based on interpretations of actions, and not on phonetic substitutions; therefore, they still did not constitute a full decipherment.

According to Schele, it was not until "1995 [that] all the parts came together and yielded a reading" (1999:36). In that year, David Stuart's dissertation referred to T713 in its accession context:

> "*k'al* means 'to bind, fasten' in Yucatec, which would be appropriate in this particular context. The entire accession statement, with the prepositional phrase **tu-ba-hi** (*t-u-bah*, 'to, on himself') may read something similar to 'the paper headband was fasten[ed] on himself'" (1995:204).

19

Table 1: Definitions of *k'al*

Yucatecan (Barrera Vasquez 1995:367-368)		
	[1]K'AL	veinte; veintena, cuenta de veinte
	[2]K'AL	cerrar con cerradura y encerrar y atrancar y detener encerrado
	[2]K'ALAH	clausurar; encerrar, encajonar
	[4]K'AL	abrochar cosa que encaja como botones o corchetes
	[6]K'AL	armar lazo, abrochar como jubones
Ch'orti' (Wisdom 1950:83, 145)		
	k'ar	'getting, holding on, retention (as of a bad sickness)
	k'ar u ya'bich	'retention of urine (lack of flow)'
	k'ar	'opening fissure, interior of neck, throat'
Ch'orti' (Hull 2005:68)		
	-k'ar	clasificador numeral para contar un veinte de algo [palabra Antigua que casi no se usa actualmente.]

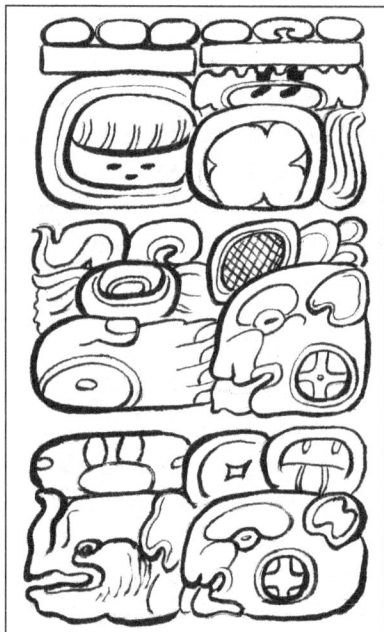

Figure 8: T713 at Palenque, from the Tablet of the Slaves. Here *k'al k'ak' huun* is followed by the phrase *tu b'aah*. T713 in various compositions. Drawings by the author after Schele (1999:36-38) and Stuart (2006:65-68)

Yet Schele attributed the actual decipherment to Werner Nahm's identification of a phonetic substitution (**k'a-la-ja**) at Chich'en Itza (1999:36). Actually, the published literature lacks clarity on this point, since Stuart's monumental article, "Kings of Stone" claims that it is the first to formally publish the decipherment.

"The *k'altun* reading deserves some comment, as it has not been published before now. In the inscriptions of Chichen Itza and northern Campeche, the hand-mirror verb is replaced by the syllabic sequence **k'a-la**, suggesting the logographic value **K'AL** (fig. 9a). In another much earlier inscription from the Bonampak region, the hand 'holds' the syllable **k'a**, where it presumably serves as a phonetic complement in **k'a-K'AL...**" (1996:155).

The determination of precedence aside, this example does reveal the rapid pace of decipherment rippling through the epigraphic community during the late 1990s and reviews some of the distinction between a glyph's syllabic decipherment and an argument for its 'meaning.'

Even the determination of its phonetic composition, though, does not settle a glyph's semantic value. Agreeing that *k'al* is the appropriate verb root, for instance, leaves us with numerous possible glosses, where we focus on Yucatecan and Ch'orti' because the latter is the closest extant language to "Classic Ch'olti'an"[4] and the former is recognized as having crept into the Dresden Codex (Lacadena 2004; Wald 2004). (Table 1)

Yet there is also considerable time depth to some of these glosses as evidenced by Terrence Kaufman's linguistic reconstruction work. (Table 2)

Table 2: Data used by Kaufman (2004) to reconstruct protoMayan *k'al

Awakateko	k'al	'lo amarro'
Itzaj	k'a"'a"li	'se cerro'
Mopan	k'aali	'se cerro'
Teko	k'aalo7	'amarrado'
Mam	k'alo7n	'amarrado'
Mam	k'alb'il	'pañuelo'
Ixil	k'alb'al	'cinturón'

Now, several of these glosses refer to 'tying,' so the intuitive appeal of *k'al sak huun* as 'tying on a white

[4] By following the practice of recognizing Classic Ch'olti'an as the language of the inscriptions, I am making a statement about the linguistic camp I am associating with, as there is still non-trivial debate on the issue. In this matter, I am most influenced by the work of John Robertson, Stephen Houston, and David Stuart, complemented by that of Alfonso Lacadena and Marc Zender.

Glyphic representation	Transcription	Analysis	Translation
	U-K'AL-wa-TUUN-ni	*u-k'al-aw tuun*	he binds the stone
	U-K'AL-TUUN-ni-li 13-AJAW 13 CHAK-AT-ta	*u-k'al-tuun-il Uxlahun Ajaw Uxlahun te' Chakat*	it is the stone-binding of 13 Ajaw 13 Woh
	i-K'AL-ja/AJ	*'i-k'a[h]laj*	'then it is tied'

Figure 9: Analysis of various uses of the *k'al* verb root (Stuart 2006:65-68).
Also, Kettunen and Helmke have **K'AL-wi** as *k'al-(aa)w-0* (2009:60)

headband,' and Stuart's persuasive 'stone-binding' reading of *k'altuun* (1996) have led to a general acceptance of *k'al* as 'to tie, to bind' (Lacadena 2004:174; Robertson *et al.* 2004:266; Stuart 2007).

Since the early 1990s, though, the sophistication of the linguistic analysis of Mayan hieroglyphic writing has increased substantially (Wichmann 2004:1-2). Accordingly, each specific record of *k'al* can now be recognized as falling into distinct categories, differing in detail. (See Figure 9) Each difference, in turn, corresponds to a form that is reconstructable (and meaningful) from Mayan linguistic analyses. The verb root has been identified as a transitive CVC (consonant-vowel-consonant) root, with common representation as **u-K'AL-wa** for *u k'alaw* (3SA tie-[TRANS]-3SB) 's/he ties it.' As for the other of its more frequent forms—including that in the Dresden Codex Venus pages—**K'AL** takes the **-ja** suffix, which Alfonso Lacadena has read as a passive intransitive derived from a CVC-transitive root (2004:174). Linguistically precedent to contemporary Ch'orti', this

requires an infixed *-h-*, yielding *k'ahlaj* 'it is tied.'[5] Even esoteric forms of the verb fit within this paradigm. With **K'AL-wi** representing an antipassive form, *k'alaaw*, 's/he tied' (Kettunen and Helmke 2009:83).

We may therefore take these results and apply them to a transcription of the text in the Dresden Codex Venus pages in an attempt to update Schele's and Grube's work.

This would yield, on Page 48, for example: **K'AL-ja la-K'IN-ni ta-wi-si-ka-la CHAK EK'**, or *k'a[h]l-aj-Ø lak'in Tawiskal Chak Ek'*, or tie-[PASS]-3SA east-[LOC] Tawiskal Chak Ek', 'is tied *to the* East Tawiskal-Venus' (where Tawiskal is recognized as a Mayanization of the Nahuatl Tlahuizcalpantecuhtli (Taube and Bade 1991:14; Whittaker 1986)).

---

[5] Much of the literature contains examples following the Yucatec that read –**aj** as a completive marker for an intransitive verb, yielding *k'alaj* as 'it was tied.'

Two qualifying notes are important here. First, although it was very common in the Classic period inscriptions to simply utilize the phrase u-ti, *uht*, 'it happened [at]' after the description of an event, the sentential position within the phrase could have provided the same meaning (Lacadena, personal communication, 2008). Second, the verb *k'ahlaj* in the Venus pages is marked for the third person singular absolutive (**K'AL-ja-Ø**). This grammatically suggests that the particular entity 'tied' should be singular. Based on this logic, we might be persuaded that "Tawiskal" (and the other deity names) should be a name for Chak Ek' supporting Thompson's interpretation over Seler's, and lending credence to the statement by Harvey Bricker and Victoria Bricker that "[t]he text says that Tlahuizcalpantecuhtli *is* Venus" (2007:108; original emphasis). Whether or not we adhere to the latter emphasis, though, it would make sound linguistic sense for us to read *k'ahlaj lak'in Kaktonal Chak Ek'* as 'Kaktonal (an aspect of) Chak Ek' is tied to the East.'

4.1 THE RIFT

Grammatically, then, there has been significant development in the linguistic understanding of the phrase in the Dresden Codex Venus pages, although it is certainly not as storied as that behind its astronomical unpacking. On the other hand, these analyses leave us with the relatively straightforward question of whether or not 'being tied in the East' is the same thing as 'appearing in the East.'

Clearly, if this were the only ambiguity within the Venus pages, then we might well consider it insignificant and let it go.[7] There is, however, a larger obstacle that must be overcome if we accept either (or both) of these readings. Specifically, if we accept the interpretation that these *k'al* phrases grammatically or astronomically identify these deities as Venus, then the text within the Venus pages becomes inconsistent on a larger level.

The problem arises because Venus is not just 'tied to the East;' it is tied sequentially to the North, West, and South as well. Each page has Venus associated with a *k'al* event in each of the four cosmological regions, and in each one, a different deity name is paired with Chak Ek'. This much is evident from Figures 2 and 3, and was recognized by Förstemann and Seler over a hundred years ago. If we follow the logic of the traditional model, this would identify Venus with different deities in each

cosmic region. As noted above, though, a complication arises in that there is only one column on each page dedicated to the other directions, yet there are two *k'ahlaj lak'in* statements describing Venus in the East. And the planet Chak Ek' is paired with different deities in each of these statements. (See Figure 2 and 3)

This point requires clarity: it is not simply that at different periods (i.e. on different pages or in different cosmological regions) Venus is "named" as a different deity. Rather, for the same period, for the same *k'al* event, say on Page 46, Chak Ek' 'is tied' or 'appears' in the East as God A (Kimil) *and* as God L.

The idea that these two passages refer to different events would run counter to all consensus in the literature thus far. For one thing, visibility in the East (corresponding to morning appearance) is cross-culturally attested within the Postclassic, as the most important. Seler made use of this observation early on as the glue holding his interpretation together. Furthermore the textual layout in the Dresden Codex seems to bear this out. On the right hand side of each page in between the spearthrower figure and the upper illustration, the text reads: **K'AL-ja la-K'IN-ni X CHAK EK' Z u-HUL u-mu-ka** …, which we may convert to *k'ahlaj lak'in X Chak Ek'. Z u hul. U mu'k* … and, if we follow the above reading for the function of *k'al*, the passage translates as: 'X (as) Venus is tied to the East. Z is speared. It is the omen of …' where the final elided portion provides a series of entities/concepts to whom the omens pertain.

So the text itself appears to provide nice corroboration of what scholars have inferred about the Venus pages, matching the pattern shown in Figure 6 (Schele and Grube 1997:141-157). That is, just as in Thompson's co-opted interpretation of the *Anales de Cuauhtitlan*: when Venus first rises in the East as Morningstar, he spears a victim, and that spearing produces an omen. That is precisely how current interpretations would have us see the Borgia Codex images, and that is precisely how tradition would have us see the images painted on pages 46 – 50 of the Dresden Codex; Venus is portrayed as a warrior holding spears and a spear thrower, and below him, a spear runs through the middle of his victim.

And so, the problem. If the deity name preceding Venus in these passages actually gives the name of Venus for that time period (or that event), then we would expect the two names given to be the same—or at least compatible. Instead, we have the result shown in Table 3.

Now we might be tempted to dismiss this complication through some suggestion that deities are thought to take on more than one aspect.[8] In the Dresden Codex, for example, the name of God L is assigned to different looking figures as can be seen in Figure 10. Perhaps this is an example of deities taking on multiple personas.

---

[6] There is actually a column drift in representation of these figures. While the middle and lower images correspond with the text above them, the upper images are shifted one page from the text in column 4 of the table of dates. So, for example, the Star Caiman name shows up in column 4 of Page 50, but the upper image of the Star Camian referent is on Page 46.

[7] Another option would be to follow Lloyd Anderson's suggestion that **K'AL** here reflects the semantic value of the K'iche' *qal* – 'to appear,' 'to manifest' (personal communication, 2008). Another possibility is that the same glyph means different things in different places. The ubiquity of *k'al* values as 'to bind' or 'to enclose' throughout Mayan languages, however, along with the argument in the rest of this article suggest otherwise.

[8] This is not unlike the argument made by Gillespie and Joyce, who show that any given representation likely is a combination of multiple deities p. 17: (1998).

Table 3: Deity names paired with Chak Ek' for identical phrases governed by the verb root *k'al*[6]

	Page 46	Page 47	Page 48	Page 49	Page 50
LHS fourth column	Kimil (God A)	4 Pawatun	Ix Uh Ajaw	Jun Ajaw	(Star Cayman)
RHS middle passage	God L	Lajun Chan	Tawiskal	Chak Xiwitel	Kaktonal

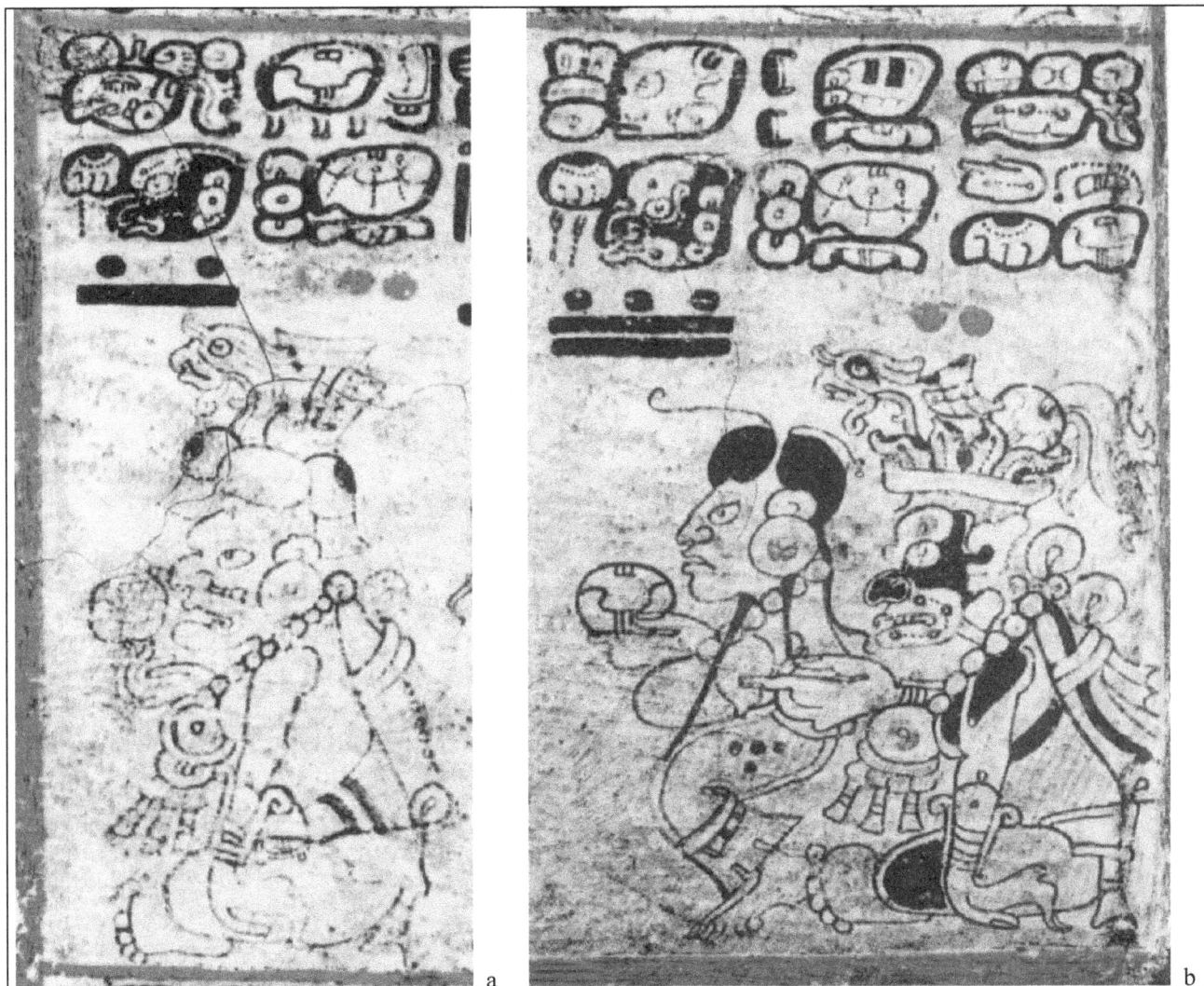

Figure 10: Different representations of God L (as identified by his name glyph in the second row, first column) in the Dresden Codex (images from the Förstemann facsimile obtained from www.famsi.org). Analysis of various uses of the *k'al* verb root (Stuart 2006:65-68). Also, Kettunen and Helmke have **K'AL-wi** as *k'al-(aa)w-0* (2009:60)

Yet the specific deities that Chak Ek' would have to become under this approach requires more significant concern. On page 48, for example, the phrase in column 4 is *k'ahlaj lak'in Ix Uh Ajaw Chak Ek'* – or 'the Moon Goddess as an aspect of Venus is tied to the East,' while that in the right-hand-side middle passage is *k'ahlaj lak'in Tawiskal Chak Ek'* – 'Tawiskal as an aspect of Venus is tied to the East.' Multiple aspects? Maybe. Venus as the Moon Goddess and the Central Mexican god of frost? Not likely.[9]

Perhaps just as perplexing, the purported name of Venus on Page 50, Kaktunal, also shows up in the lower register of text on Page 47. Here, though, the text reads… *u muk ? u muk Kaktunal.* That is the omen, *u muuk*, generated by the spearing of Chak B'ahlam by Venus-as-Lahun Chan is the omen of another purported identity of Venus.

These conflations are further exemplified by the role of the Maize God in the Venus Table. On Page 48, the Maize God is the speared victim, occupying the lower image register. On Page 50, the Maize God shows up in the first column as the 'aspect of Venus tied to the North' *and* as the patient of an omen for the *k'al* and spearing events of the East. (See Figure 11)

[9] Granted, there is something odd going on here as noted above since the images of the deities named in the LHS fourth column are placed on the following page (i.e. Ix Uh Ajaw is named on page 48, but depicted at the top of page 49), but this does not provide a simple solution to the problem of identities, and in any case, the solution proposed below makes better sense of it.

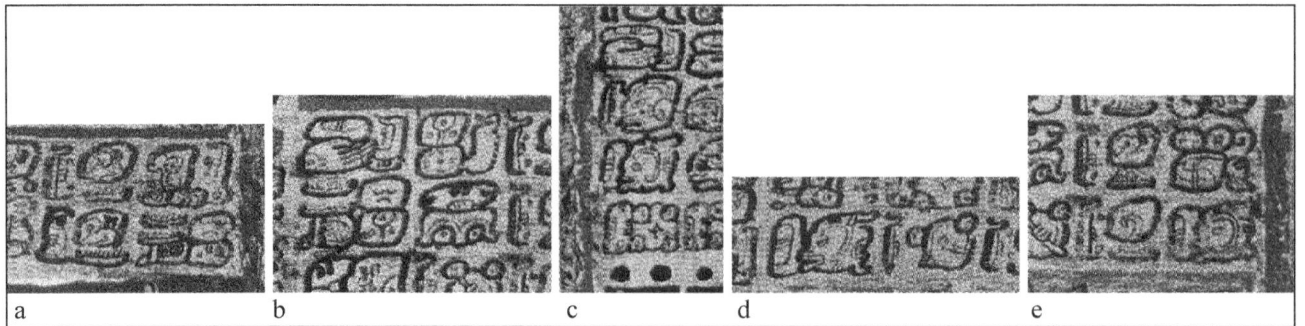

Figure 11: Deities bound with Chak Ek' showing up in other contexts: a) u muuk Kaktunal 'Kaktunal's omen' (p. 47); b) k'ahlaj lak'in Kaktunal Chak Ek' (p. 50); c) k'ahlaj xaman [Maize God] Chak Ek' (p. 50); d) [Maize God] is speared (p. 48); e) u muuk [Maize God] 'it is the Maize God's omen' (p. 50) (images from the Förstemann facsimile obtained from www.famsi.org)

Now it is not impossible that the issue here is merely conceptual; it may result from a failure of our ability to *translate* Mayan astronomical concepts and not from a problem with the scholarship per se. On the other hand, I suggest that there is yet another "small" problem with current interpretations that we must contend with, and which, together with this one, leads to an alternative reading that makes more straightforward sense of the interactions and relationships among the various deities of the Venus Table. First, though, we turn to this other complication.

Chapter 2:
EXTERNAL APPEAL, THE THIRD DOLL

One of the troubles plaguing the interpretation of the Dresden Codex Venus Table has been its lack of provenance information. Without a specific geographic context for the manuscript, we are left looking for other means of contextualizing the document and its contents. I argue here that an illuminating context comes from the recognition that the verb root in question, *k'al*, also corresponds to the only currently known explicit narrative reference to Venus from the Classic period.[10] (See Figure 12)

Within a narrative taking up eight inscriptions on the walls of the temple atop Copan Structure 10L-11, we confront this unique Venus record. By recognizing that the narrative contains explicit astronomical events recorded along with historical events, we will find new evidence that the patron of this text, Yax Pahsaj Chan Yop At, went to great pains to integrate cosmological themes into this temple. While scholars have recognized this within the architectural imagery for some time (Fash 1991:168; Miller 1988; Newsome 2001:50-51), this section demonstrates the theme on subtler levels.

Beyond the more complex reading of Temple 11, the reading presented here takes us back to reveal a second problem with modern interpretations of the Dresden Codex Venus Table—this one calendric. Fortunately, there is substantial reward for taking up this problem: the resolution provides a more coherent reading of the Preface to the Venus Table and a new solution to the meaning of the 1.5.5.0 interval.

3.4 CONCEPTUAL CONTINUITY ACROSS THE CLASSIC-POSTCLASSIC

Thanks to the Peabody Museum excavations at Copan initiated in 1891, Structure 10L-11 enjoys a much richer

contextualization than the Dresden Codex. Patronized by Yax Pahsaj Chan Yop At, the sixteenth member of the ruling dynasty, the structure was built in a liminal position architecturally, separating the main public plaza that enveloped the primary ball court from the more private royal buildings known today as the acropolis (Fash 1991:166; 1998:254-255). (See Figure 13) The entire structure carried heavy cosmic imagery, extending into the temple at the top of this pyramid (Fash 1991:168; Fash and Fash 1996:138; Schele and Freidel 1990:322-328). The upper temple was oriented such that two halls crossed at the center of the temple and terminated in doorways, opening out onto the four cosmological regions (Schele and Freidel 1990:326). In turn, each exit bore hieroglyphic inscriptions on both of its walls, yielding the aforementioned eight texts. While the architecture will concern us below, we move now to consider the content of the inscriptions to establish its relevance to the Dresden Codex Venus Table.

Well within David Stuart's characterization of the hieroglyphic inscriptions of Copan (1996), the overall content of these texts is anything but mundane. The narrative does start, intuitively enough, on the North exit East wall (NE) with a statement of the patron's accession: [JGU] **9 PIH 16 WINIK-HAAB 12 HAAB 5 WINIK 17 K'IN-ni ti** [6 KABAN] [G9] **10 MOL 11/12 HUL-ya** [6Cs] **UH-10 JOY-AJAW-le YAX-pa-sa CHAN-na YOP-AT-ta K'UHUL-AJAW-**[Copan], '9.16.12.5.17 6 Kaban 10 Mol. G9. Eleven (or 12) days earlier the 6th Death Moon arrived. It was a 30-day moon. Yax Pahsaj Chan Yop At, K'uhulajaw of Copan was bound in rulership.'

The overall narrative continues by hopping back and forth between the rule of Waxaklajun Ub'aah K'awiil, Copan's thirteenth k'uhulajaw, and the patron's own contemporary events. (See Figure 12) The two hops of particular interest for this essay are on the East exit North wall (EN), East exit South wall (ES) and West exit North wall (WN).

---
[10] There is some inconsistency in the literature concerning what constitutes a Venus record. For a full discussion, see Aldana (2005).

25

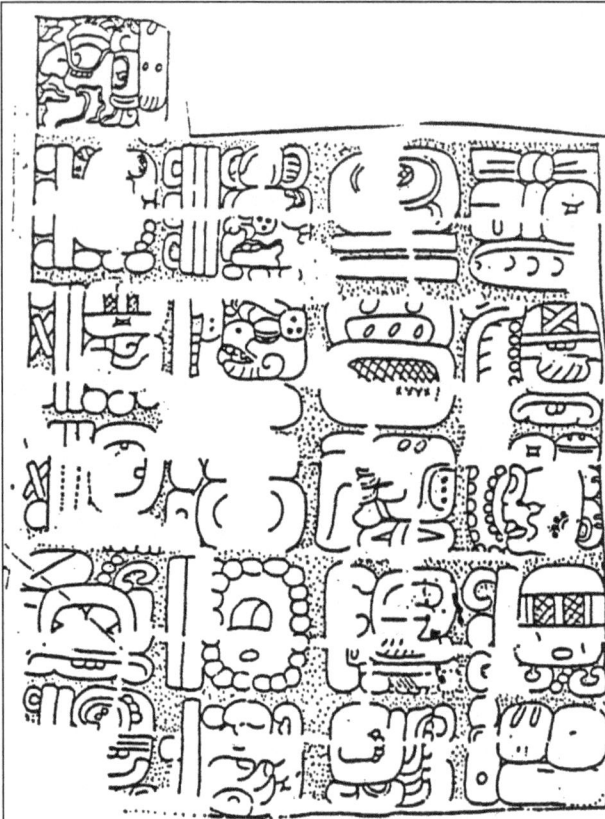

a

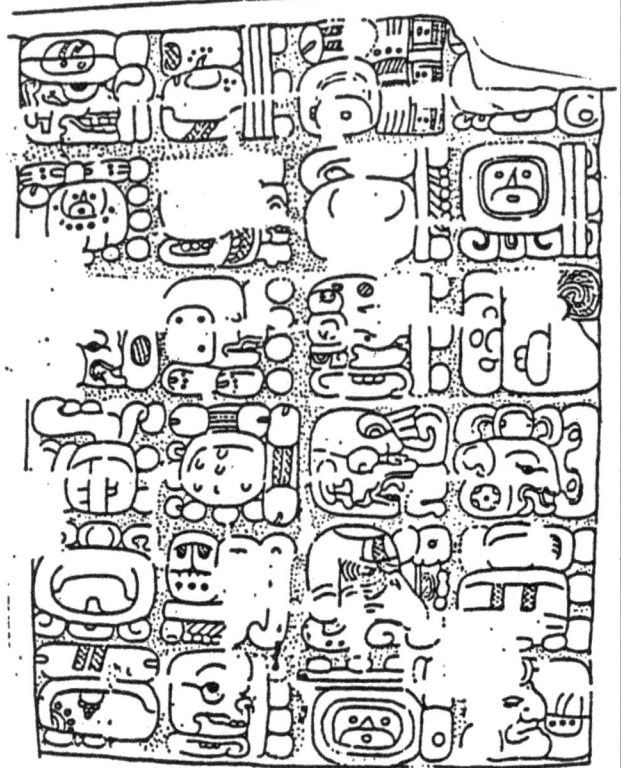

c

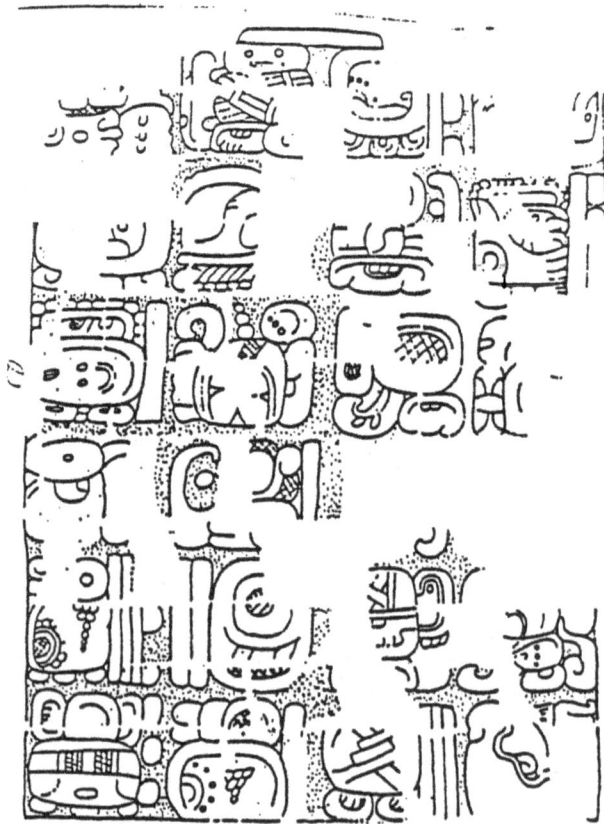

b

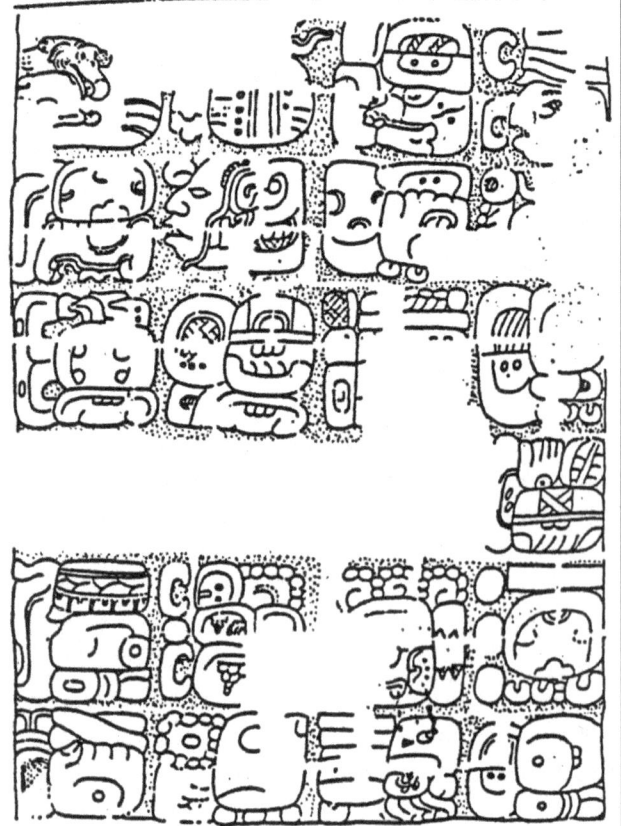

d

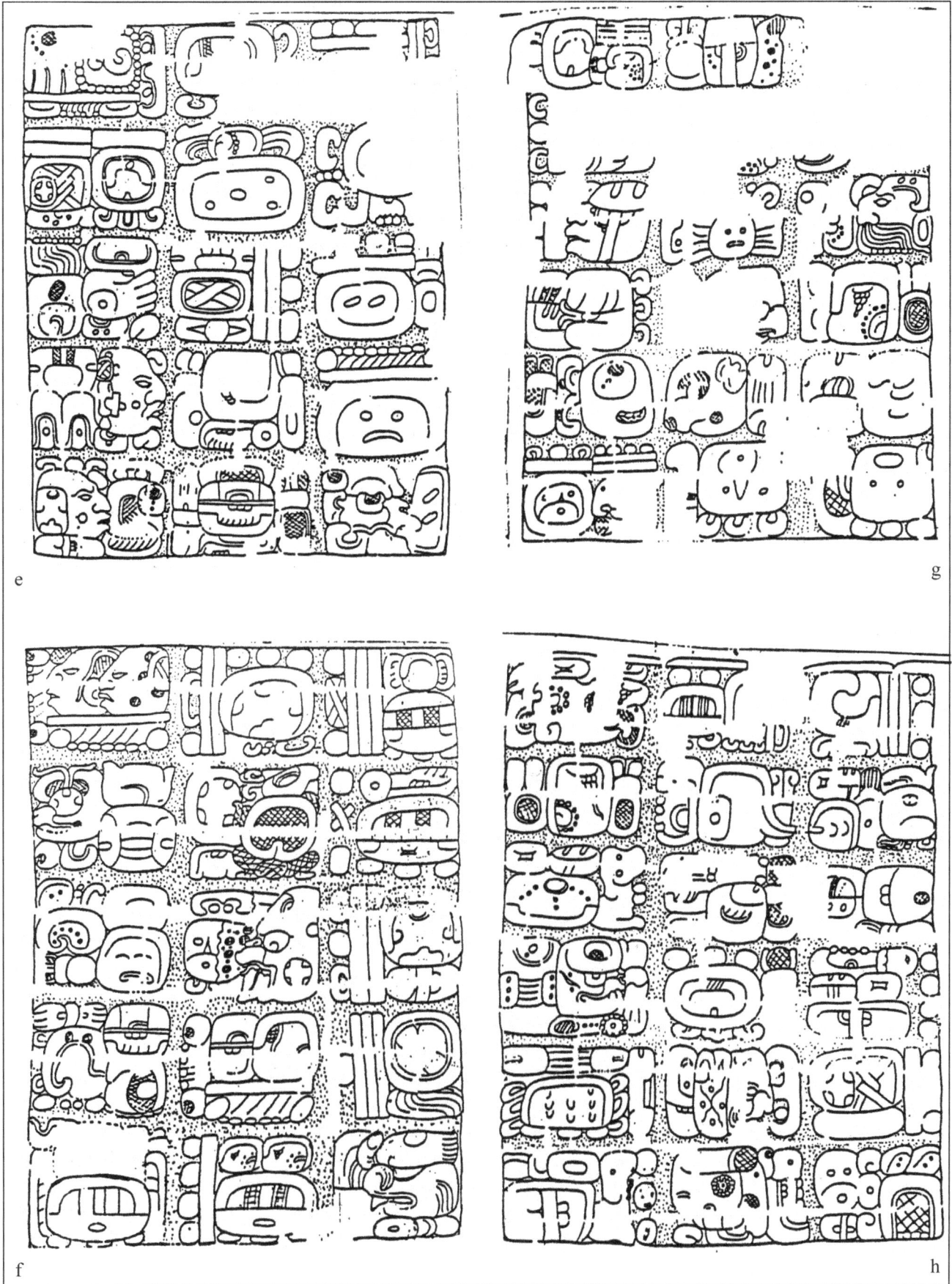

Figure 12: Illustrations of the inscriptions in the doorways of Structure 10L-11 at Copan, Honduras
Drawing by Linda Schele, © David Schele, courtesy Foundation for the Advancement
of Mesoamerican Studies, Inc., www.famsi.org

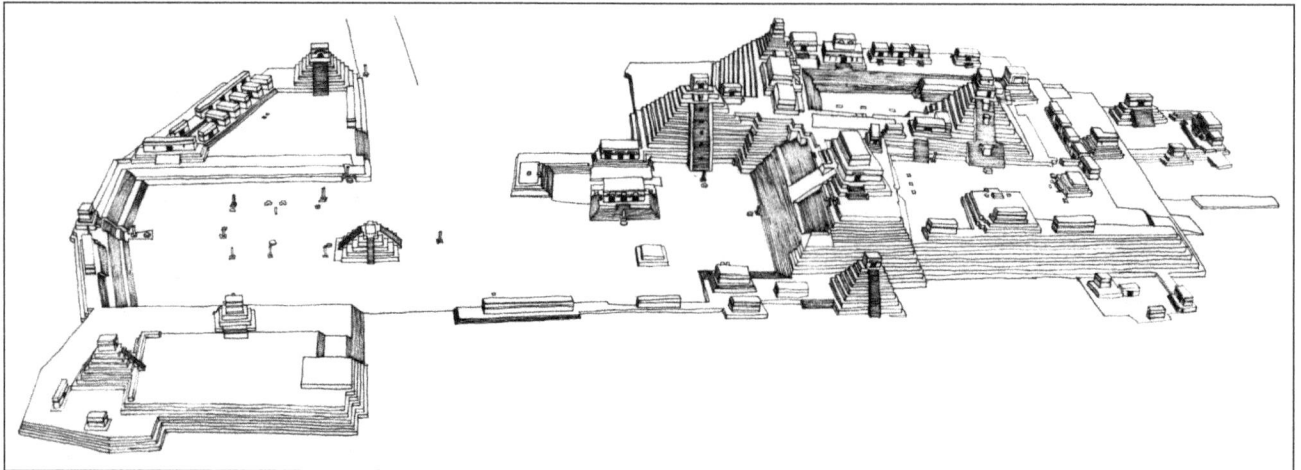

Figure 13: Schele's reconstruction of Copan during the Late Classic. Structure 10L-11 is the large building to the right of center; it faces north toward the ballcourt and the length of the open plaza. Drawing by Linda Schele, © David Schele, courtesy Foundation for the Advancement of Mesoamerican Studies, Inc., www.famsi.org

The EN wall begins with the phrase *u tz'akaj* ('to arrange,' 'to put in order' (Mathews and Bíro 2008)), which is used throughout the eight tablets to break up the narrative according to events separate in time. A Calendar Round (anchoring the event at least to one date every 52 years) follows; here, it is 5 Kib 10 Pop. Next is the verb root we saw in the Dresden Codex, *k'al*, followed by the titled name of Venus: **AJAW-wa CHAK EK'**. (See Figure 12, East Exit, North Wall)

When it comes to the verb here, the suffixation differs from that of the Dresden Codex passages. Admittedly, this is one of the less frequent forms in which we find this verb, taking –**wa**, –**ni**, and –**yi** suffixes.[11] Helping in this regard, the suffixation is relatively common for the verb root *chum*, 'to sit.' John Robertson, Stephen Houston, and David Stuart have argued that –**wa** and –**ni** combine to generate the linguistic predecessor to the Ch'orti' positional marker –*wan* (2004:266; Stuart 2006:64). Accordingly, **CHUM-wa-ni** becomes *chumwan* 's/he sits.' Furthermore, the final -**ya** serves as a completive aspect marker yielding *chumwaniiy*, 's/he sat.'[12] Accordingly, at Copan, we should read the verb as *k'alwaniiy*, 's/he was in a tied position.'

At first blush, this seems to match the traditional interpretation. While it does not specify a cosmic region, it does note that in Yax Pahsaj's past, Ajaw Chak Ek' 'was in a tied position.' At some level, then, it does imply a continuity in astronomical conceptualization between the Late Classic at Copan and the Postclassic records in the Dresden Codex (i.e. a Venus event is recorded with the same verb root *k'al*). This continuity becomes stronger when we consider more of the Structure 10L-11 narrative.

The Venus record on the EN wall is followed immediately by another *u tz'akaj* phrase, this one introducing the 819-day count station of ES. I have argued elsewhere that the 819-day count was a tool invented at Palenque for the computation of astrologically and numerologically relevant dates within historical narratives (Aldana 2001:135-192, 2002, 2007; see also Powell 1997:12-20). Such a tool would fit perfectly with the rest of the content of these tablets, as we will see. At the very least, though, scholars agree that the count carries an esoteric calendric meaning and makes a cosmic course through the North, West, South, and East (Thompson 1975:212-217; Lounsbury 1978:773-774).

The 819-day count record in turn is a quick stop on the way to an (unorthodoxly placed) explicit Long Count 9.17.2.12.16. There is a nearly full Supplementary Series here (Glyphs G, F, X, C, and A), but in this case, the record "skips" the moon age (Glyphs D and E), instead giving the moon's name (Glyph X), its numerological position (Glyph C), and the attendant "Lord of the Night" (Glyphs G and F).[13] Given the enormous amount of lunar data in the corpus of hieroglyphic inscriptions, though, and Yax Pahsaj's introductory Long Count, we can readily compute that 9.17.2.12.16 should have corresponded to a New Moon.[14] This, in fact, is what the rest of the text tells us as well.

In any case, the unorthodoxy of Glyph D's and E's absence can be explained by the next hieroglyphic passage: **i-IL-ji** [eroded glyph block] **tu- UH NAH ch'o-ko**, or *i[h]l-[a]j ? t(i) Uh nah. Ch'ok.* See-[PASS]-3SA PREP Moon House. Sprout-[INTR]-3SA. These two

---

[11] The verb **K'AL-wa-ni-ya** also shows up at Palenque in K'an B'ahlam's Triad Group. The context is rather obscure, however, and will be taken up explicitly in another essay.

[12] The difference between –**ya** and –**yi** as the final syllable follows the pattern noted by Lacadena that the rules of disharmonious vowel length break down during the Late Classic (2006). See also Hruby and Childe (2006).

[13] For more on the Supplementary Series, see below, or Thompson (1972).

[14] The Initial Series date from the East wall of the North exit gives 9.16.12.5.17 as a Moon Age of 11 (possibly 12). The difference between 9.17.2.12.16 and 9.16.12.5.17 is 10.6.19 or 3,739 days. Using a synodic moon of 29.53 days, this puts 9.17.2.12.16 18 days after the Moon Age of the earlier date, i.e. 11 + 18 = 29. Twenty-nine days after a Moon Age of '0' is effectively another Moon Age of '0' or New Moon. Also, reference recent articles on Lunar Series.

Table 4: Parallel narratives in the inscription of Copan Structure 10L-11

	Past	Intermediate	Contemporary
Astronomical	Venus	819-Day Count station	New Moon
Historical	Waxaklajun Ub'aah K'awiil	9.17.0.0.0 Period End	Dedication of Structure 10L-11

sentences are the actual event corresponding to the date 1 Kib 19 Keh. They are immediately followed by a new date and another event.

While the first sentence is interesting: "Someone/Something is seen PREP the Moon house," the second is key. Most commonly within the hieroglyphic corpus, *ch'ok* seems to be used as a title for young nobility ("*ch'ok* – adj. unripe, young;" "n. title which designates heirs to the throne (not exclusively)" (Mathews and Bíro 2005). In this case, though, *ch'ok* is especially interesting relative to what we know from Ch'orti'. Kerry Hull has recently put together a wonderfully useful "abbreviated dictionary" of Ch'orti' terms along with their usage in sentences. One such example uncannily matches our needs.

ch'ok katu' luna tierna (new moon)

E katu' numuy sajmi. Ejk'ar ch'ok. Hoy pasó la luna. Mañana estará tierna. (The moon passed this morning. Tomorrow it will be a new moon.) (Hull 2005).

Notice that the second sentence comprises only the term for 'tomorrow' (*ejk'ar*) and the term *ch'ok*. In the C'horti' case, *ch'ok* by itself should be 'it is/will be new moon.' And that is precisely what we confront in the Copan case: 'X is seen PREP the Moon house. It is New Moon.'

By itself, then, this is a very nice lunar record; relative to the rest of the text, the passage serves a larger purpose. We may now recognize the narrative of the EN, ES, and WN walls as recording an explicit Venus event, an 819-day count station, and then an explicit Moon event. This is a self-contained set of astronomical statements. Unlike other arguments for planetary references in hieroglyphic inscriptions (Aveni 2001:167-169; Dütting and Aveni 1982; Dütting 1985; Tate 1985; Closs 1994; Aldana 2007), we do not need to infer astronomy behind a cloak of patterns among dates here. These are explicit.

Yet it is tremendously useful to place this astronomical narrative in its greater context. The set of eight texts began with a record of Yax Pahsaj Chan Yop At's accession on the first wall (NE). The next passage reaches into the historic past, 3 k'atuns earlier, to record the events of Ruler 13, Waxaklajun Ub'aah K'awiil. Next, the text notes the 9.17.0.0.0 Period End, on its way to recording the first instance of the Calendar Round 1 Kib 19 Keh, corresponding to 9.17.2.12.16—the dedication of the building itself.

As shown in Table 4, the two trajectories are parallel. Even more provocative, they arrive at the same terminus. The astronomical narrative ends on the New Moon that occurred on 1 Kib 19 Keh, the same date as the *och k'ahk'* event of the historical sequence.

The final event of the whole narrative concerns the Mo' Ajaw, Mo' Wits Ajaw, is associated with the ancient name of Copan, Ux Witik, and ties together both narrative threads. This final event accomplishes the latter by continuing the historical thread, while advancing the astronomical story. This time, though, the astronomy does become "subtext." Here we must look below the surface of the text and compute differences between dates recorded to see the astronomical aspect.[15]

The final event transpires on 9.17.0.0.16, recorded by the Calendar Round 3 Kib 9 Pop. The binding of this historical record to its astronomical reflection occurs in the recognition that 9.17.0.0.16:

1. was exactly 15 Venus Rounds after the explicit Venus record treated above (9.17.0.0.16 – 9.15.15.12.16 = 8,760 = 15 x 584);

2. was the first full moon of the eighteenth k'atun (winikhaab); *and*

3. was the twenty-fourth *haab* anniversary of the Venus event.

Moreover, it is interesting to note that if the Copan scribe who authored this inscription were consulting a manuscript like the Dresden Codex, this interval from 5 Kib to 3 Kib would have corresponded to a move downward of three rows in the table of 260-day count dates. (See Figure 14) Therefore, the manuscript itself would have explicitly recorded both events as *k'al* events in the same cosmic region.

Overall, then, the inscriptions of Copan Str. 10L-11 provide significant evidence for continuity in Venus records across the Classic/Postclassic divide. Now there are some oddities within these tablets, but they are not without supported resolution. Here, we will consider the visual, calendric, and distributional abnormalities in the Temple 11 inscriptions.

The first anomaly is that many of the glyphs are "backwards." That is, most hieroglyphs in the writing

---

[15] This method is directly parallel to the methods used in the cosmological texts of Palenque patronized by Kan B'ahlam and his eventual successor, Ak'ahl Mo' Naab'. The full argument along with supporting data is presented in *The Apotheosis of Janaab' Pakal* (2007).

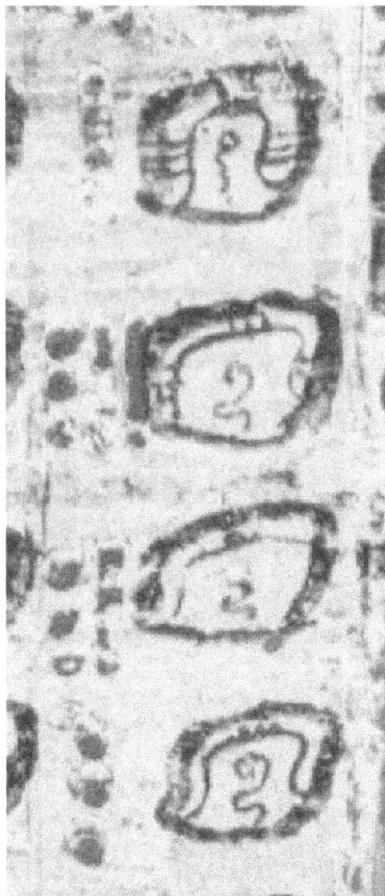

Figure 14: Jump from 5 Kib to 3 Kib in the Dresden Codex Venus Table (image from the Förstemann facsimile obtained from www.famsi.org)

Figure 15: Yaxchilan Lintel 25, showing reversed glyph orientation (Photograph K2888 © Justin Kerr)

system are asymmetrical and possess a conventional orientation. (Compare Figures 2 & 12) For four of the eight texts in Structure 10L-11 (NW, SE, EN, and WS), the standard orientation is reversed (Fash 1991:168; Schele and Freidel 1990:326-327). Schele and Freidel suggest that this was a visual pun intended for 'the gods' (1990:327). This break with convention was not unique, however, as it was also utilized by Itzamnaah B'ahlam, Late Classic ruler of Pa'chan (Yaxchilan). Also in a doorway, Lintel 25 (Structure 23) possessed the "mirrored" image shown in Figure 15 (Fash 1991:168; Tate 1992:119-121, 204-208). Thus some of the glyph orientations are odd, but they are not without precedence in the corpus of Mayan hieroglyphic writing. In fact here, there is a reasonable suggestion, as we will see next, that the texts were oriented in this way so that they would "face out" of the structure onto the four cosmic regions.

Another unorthodoxy of the Temple 11 inscriptions is that the reading order from one wall to the next is not "linear." That is, in order to read these texts 'in order,' 'in succession' (as the glyphs themselves require (*u tz'ak*)), we must follow an interesting pattern. Specifically, the narrative covers its historical theme by starting in the NE, then moving to the NW before crossing through the center of the temple, and continuing with the SE wall and concluding with the SW wall. The astronomical theme is picked up on the EN wall, and then continued in mirrored

fashion, proceeding to the ES, before passing through the center of the temple, and then finishing with the WN and then the WS walls. (See Figure 16) The tablet order thus carries the reader through intersecting loops, symmetric about a NE/SW axis. Although it may seem eccentric, we will find good reason for this pattern in the discussion below on cosmology.

The final oddity in the 10L-11 tablets at Copan is that the Calendar Round date for the Venus event noted above does not match convention. The text unambiguously records the Calendar Round 5 Kib 10 Pop. The problem here is with the coefficient of the haab date. Because there are 20 day signs in the *chol qiij* and 365 days in a haab, each day sign may only coincide with one of four coefficients for any given month.[16] During the Classic period, the day signs were restricted to haab coefficients as shown in Table 5. Accordingly, the Calendar Round date recorded at Copan would have been 5 Kib 9 Pop to match the Classic period convention.

There are two issues to consider in resolving this break with convention. The first is that this is neither an isolated case at Copan nor is it unique for this ruler's patronized inscriptions. On the WN wall of Temple 11, for example, the Calendar Round recorded is 6 Ajaw 14 K'ayab. Again, according to the Classic period

---

[16] 365 mod 20 = 5; 20/5 = 4 → 4 Day Sign-Haab Coefficient pairs

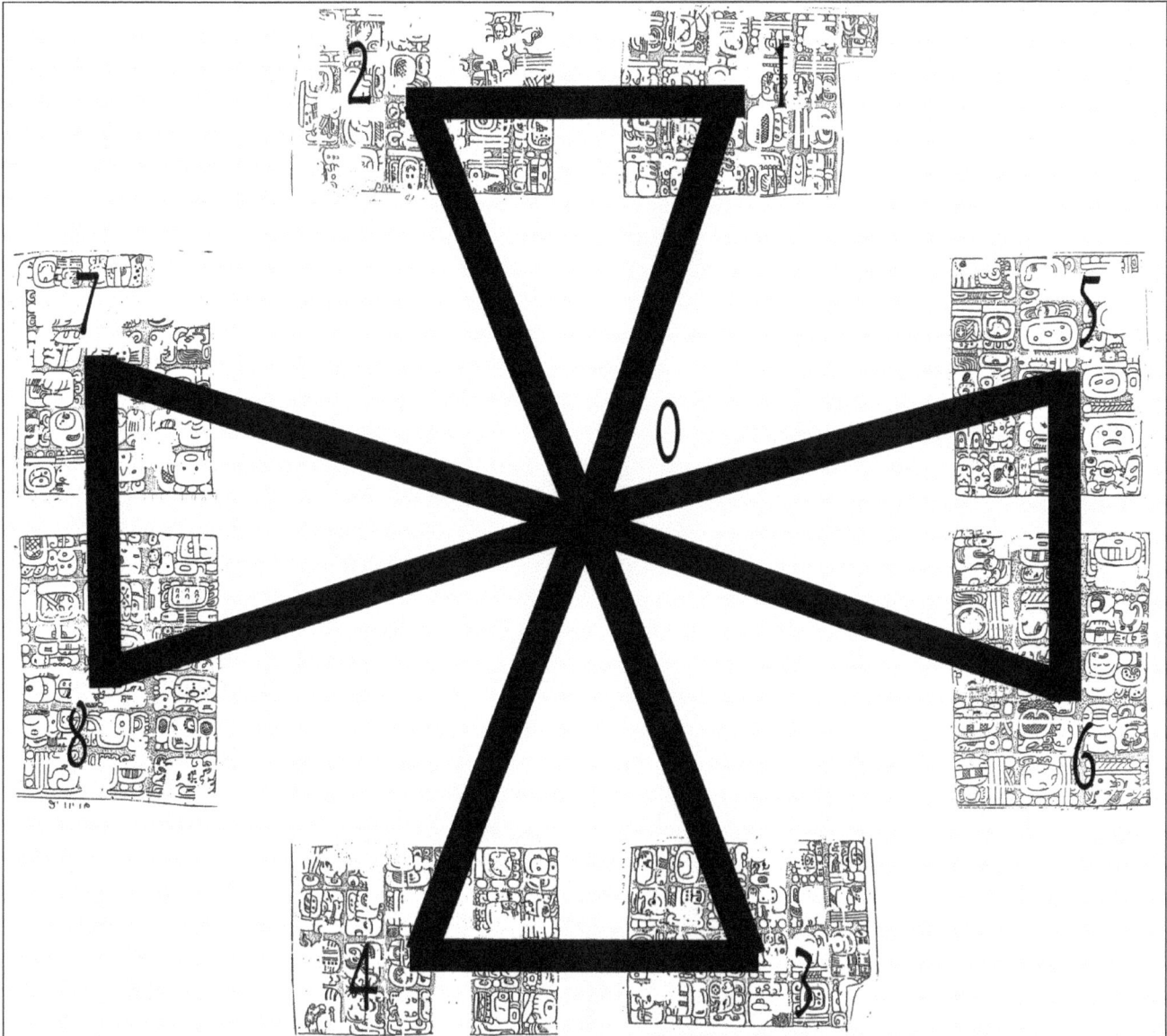

Figure 16: Pattée cross pattern followed in order to read sequentially the inscriptional
narrative within Copan Structure 10L-11

Table 5: Day Sign – *Haab* correlation during the Classic
period

Day Signs	Conventional Classic Period Haab Coefficients
Imix, Kimi, Chuwen, Kib	4, 9, 14, 19
Ik', Manik, Eb, Kaban	0, 5, 10, 15
Ak'bal, Lamat, Ben, Etz'nab	1, 6, 11, 16
K'an, Muluk, Ix, Kawak	2, 7, 12, 17
Chikchan, Ok, Men, Ajaw	3, 8, 13, 18

convention, this should have been 6 Ajaw 13 K'ayab. The latter clearly would have corresponded to 9.17.5.0.0, an appropriate Period End for the context, and one agreed upon by others as the referent for the Calendar Round recorded on Altar Q as we will see next (Schele and Freidel 1990:324). Two such unconventional dates within

the same narrative suggests that this was probably not just a careless mistake.

The point is made further by another example, the one occurring on Altar Q—that modern and ancient symbol of the Copan dynasty—located in front of Structure 10L-16, within the same court as Structure 10L-11, and patronized by the same ruler. Here, the date of the dynastic founder's, Yax K'uk' Mo''s, arrival at Ux Witik, is immediately followed by seventeen k'atuns, transporting us into the time period of Ruler 16, Yax Pahsaj Chan Yop At. On this date, Yax Pahsaj dedicated the founder's altar on the same period end noted above (**6 AJAW 13 K'AYAB** [9.17.5.0.0] **T'AB-yi ya-**[altar] **K'INICH YAX K'UK' MO', u-K'AB-ji-ya YAX PASAHJ CHAN-na YOPAAT-ti**). A distance number of **3 WINIK** and **4 K'IN** follows, leading to 5 KIB 13 WO, on which date **u-CH'AM te-**[altar] – 'he received the altar.' The latter date (5 Kib 13 Wo) mathematically "should" have been 9.17.5.3.4 5 Kib 12 Wo. (See Figure

Figure 17: Replica of Yax Pahsaj Chan Yopaat's hieroglyphic text carved into Altar Q,
which stands in front of Copan Structure 10L-16

17). Again though we confront a one-day shift in the haab coefficient. The advancement of the haab coefficient by one day relative to the 260-day count date, therefore, seems to have held some meaning for Yax Pahsaj Chan Yop At.

The second issue speaking to the break with calendric convention relates to Peter Mathews's consideration of other Calendar Round "mismatches" at Dos Pilas and Yaxchilan. Mathews's provocative hypothesis is that these dates were intentionally mismatched, reflecting Mayan time-keeping practices (2001:406). Specifically, if the 260-day count and the haab advanced at different points during a "day," then a mismatch would have reflected that liminal time when one had advanced and the other had not. (See Figure 18) Using modern hours, Mathews explains:

"it is possible that the *tzolkin* day and the *haab* day began at different times in the 24-hour day; if so, we could expect a minority of dates to be not in the 'normal' form. In other words: if, for example, the *tzolkin* day began at 6:00 P.M., and the *haab* day at 6:00 A.M., and some event took place at midnight, then the *tzolkin* date would be one position advanced with respect to the *haab* date" (Mathews 2001: 406).

David Stuart has accepted Mathews's hypothesis and extended it to incorporate a unique record at a Campeche site, Hecelchakan. Stuart reads **4-MULUK K'IN o-chi-ya tu-16-MAK** on a door lintel as:

Chan Muluk k'in
Ochiiy tu Waklajun Mak

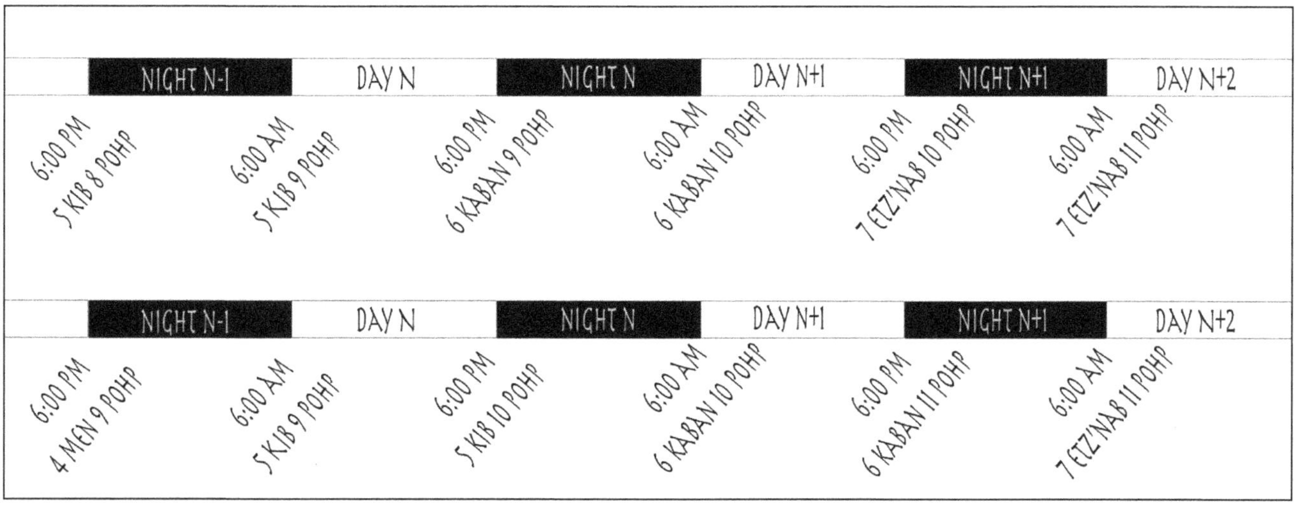

Figure 18: Two models for the non-synchronous advance of the *chol qiij* and the *haab*

Four Muluk (is) the day
It entered on the 16th of Mak
(2004:1).

He then interprets this as explicit evidence that the haab and the "tzolkin" advanced at different times of day. He goes further to suggest the possibility that the "Puuc dates" did not represent a geographic shift in calendric practice; rather he proposes that they may have been more concerned with being very precise in noting the time of day within their records (2004:2).

Eric Thompson treated a generalization of this question some decades earlier, investigating the start of the day in different areas and over different times. Perhaps not surprisingly, Thompson found evidence for local variation (1960:102). That is, Thompson reviewed ethnographic evidence that Mayan days started at sunset in Guatemala, but probably started at sunrise in Yucatan (1960:102). He wavered on specifying definitively the start of the day in the "Initial Series Period," but favored a sunrise anchor (1960:102).

Specifics aside, Thompson's observations combined with Mathews's and Stuart's suggest that local variation in time-keeping practices may have been significant. That is, it allows us to consider the more general hypothesis that mismatches reflected events transpiring 'in-between' the advances of the components of the Calendar Round, as well as the more specific hypothesis that this mechanism can explain the dates at Copan. If the day-keepers at Copan subscribed to an alternate prioritization (relative to Dos Pilas and Yaxchilan) such that the 260-day count advanced at sunrise and the haab advanced at sundown, then the record of 5 Kib 10 Pop would suggest an evening/nighttime event.

Similar local variation in astronomical practice is clearly evidenced by a comparison of Lunar Series records over time and place. Scholars since Teeple have shown that local practices and cross-regional alliances seem to find expression in the practice of counting lunar periods, i.e.

the coefficient of Glyph C (Teeple 1930; Satterthwaite 1947; Schele, Grube, and Fahsen 1992; Aldana 2006). Since the event captured by the numbering convention is arbitrary in both Glyph C and in the relative advance of the chol qiij versus the haab', the variation may well be explained by local preference.

Regardless, the repeated mismatches at least set up the hypothesis that the Calendar Round mismatches at Copan may have signaled nighttime/post-sundown events. If this was the case, then we can further hypothesize that the 5 Kib 10 Pohp mismatch suggests that that Venus event transpired at night. We also may see the two events on 9.17.5.0.0 as having occurred at different times during the 'day'—the Period End ceremony during the daytime, and the altar ceremony at night. To this hypothesis we will return below.

For now, though, it is important to recognize that a continuity does seem to exist between the Late Classic conceptualization of Venus events recorded at Copan and the early Postclassic events in the Dresden Codex. It is even possible to see the author of the Copan text consulting a manuscript in exactly the same tradition as that explicitly recorded in the Dresden manuscript.

3.3 THE GMT'S REQUISITE DISCONTINUITY

Accepting that there is a consistent aesthetic to the content, format, and "errors" within the Copan Temple 11 text, and considering its similarity to the Dresden Codex, we are compelled to ask whether there is any other evidence for continuity between the Dresden Codex and the Copan Str. 10L-11 texts. In fact, there is one more consistency that, when resolved, generates a new reading of the Dresden Codex Venus pages. Although sensible in motivation, such an exploration is not without its obstacles.

According to all modern interpretations, Page 24 of the Dresden Codex, the "Preface" of the Venus Table, tells us unequivocally that 9.9.9.16.0 1 Ajaw 18 K'ayab was an anchor for the calendrics of the entire table. Just what kind of anchor it provided, though, has been the subject of much concerted attention over the last 80 years (Teeple 1931:97-98; Thompson 1972:63-64; Lounsbury 1983, 1992a; Aveni 2001:191; Bricker and Bricker 2007).

At one level, the importance of the *chol qiij* portion of this date is not difficult to see. The Venus Table of pages 46 through 50 ends (and so begins a new cycle) on a date 1 Ajaw. (Thompson called it the *lub* in reference to a 'resting place' (1972:22, 62).) In this position, the 1 Ajaw base date of the entire table occurs as a first morning visibility event and is associated with the East. We already have seen that first morning appearance is treated preferentially within the Table, as it is in the final column of dates, and its events constitute the subject of the entire right-hand-side of each of pages 46 through 50.

On the right hand side of Page 24, the table of multiples of (5 x 584=) 2,920 also starts with an implicit 1 Ajaw anchor, as we have seen above and as can be identified in Figures 2 and 3. Furthermore, every Great Cycle recorded at the top of Page 24 takes a date 1 Ajaw to another date 1 Ajaw; and every correction interval mediates between dates 1 Ajaw as well. Finally, the Ring Number at the bottom of Page 24 starts with a date 1 Ajaw 18 K'ayab, and gets moved forward to the historical date 9.9.9.16.0 1 Ajaw 18 K'ayab. According to the principle of parsimony, then—and restricting our view only to this document—it would be most straightforward to take the 9.9.9.16.0 1 Ajaw 18 K'ayab date as an historical anchor intending to capture a heliacal rise (first morning visibility) event.

If we just stop here with the internal consistency of the manuscript, then we might be tempted to hypothesize that 9.9.9.16.0 1 Ajaw 18 K'ayab corresponded to a historically observed heliacal rise and was maintained as such into the Postclassic. If so, then it would make sense to look for a possible connection between this record in the Dresden Codex and the Venus record at Copan. That is, if both were records of historical observation, or if both came from the same ephemeris, a simple computation would bolster the historical interpretation of both dates. Especially since the author of the Copan record used the same verb root to mark Venus events as the scribe behind the Dresden Codex Venus pages and since the Copan dates recorded were separated by 15 Venus Rounds (= 3 x 2,920), we would be remiss to not check whether there was some continuity between the two dates.

In fact, the interval between 9.15.15.12.16 and 9.9.9.16.0 is 45,296 days, which in turn comprises 77 Venus Rounds and 328 days. This remainder of 328 days places the Copan record extremely close to the canonical first evening visibility station predicted by the Dresden Codex. (See Figure 19) This is close enough, if fact, that (again) we can follow a hypothetical progression through a Dresden Codex type Venus table. That is, if the Copan astronomers also recognized 9.9.9.16.0 1 Ajaw 18 K'ayab

as a canonical first morning appearance, they would have expected another first morning appearance one Great Cycle later on 9.14.15.6.0 1 Ajaw 18 K'ayab. This would take them to an expected first morning appearance on 9.15.14.14.8 2 Lamat 6 Sip (Dresden Codex, p. 47, column 4), and then to a **K'AL** event in the West on 9.15.15.12.14 3 Ix 7 Pohp (Dresden Codex, p. 48, column 2). Instead of 3 Ix 7 Pohp, though, the event at Copan was recorded as occurring two days later on 9.15.15.12.16 5 Kib 9 Pohp.

The two days between the expected event on the 3 Ix 7 Pohp and the recorded event on 5 Kib 9 Pohp fit well within astronomically conditioned expectations. That is, if the dates in the Venus Table were meant to predict exact Venus events, then we would be forced to see this as an error, and so regard the near synchronicity between the Copan record and the Dresden Codex as mere coincidence—or a near coincidence of no real import. An appeal to the actual use of the Venus Table, though, makes clear that these two days are not at all troublesome.

All studies of the Venus Table recognize that Venus events (first and last morning appearance and first and last evening appearances) are quite variable by a number of days early or late. Floyd Lounsbury made explicit use of this variability in search of a historical placement of the Venus Table (1983, 1992a). Most recently, the Brickers have taken up a similar method to argue that the Venus Table was intended as a warning table such that the dates in the table would be most effective if they *anticipated* the actual event (2007:106-107). A **K'AL** event on 9.15.15.12.16 5 Kib 10 Pohp would have perfectly matched this approach for an event predicted for 9.15.15.12.14 3 Ix 7 Pohp. Not wholly unrelated, I have argued that the dates in the Venus Table were intended as target dates, with the expectation that actual events would occur either slightly before or slightly after the predicted date (Aldana 2007). In either of these cases (and in any other published in the scholarly literature),[17] the two-day "error" fits easily within reconstructions of *the use* of the Venus Table.

Yet there is more evidence that the intent of the Copan record was to capture an observed event. For this, we return to the promised hypothesis concerning Calendar Round mismatches. That is, first evening visibility of Venus would have occurred just at/after sunset. If we recall from the last section that the date of the Copan Venus record, 5 Kib 10 Pohp may have indicated an evening event—that is, if the model for a non-synchronous advance of the chol qiij and haab is invoked—then this record is explicit that the Copan *k'al* event occurred after sunset. In other words, if we accept that the Dresden Codex anchor recorded a historical first morning visibility of Venus, then the Copan date would have corresponded to a first evening visibility, which may well have been flagged as such with a Calendar Round mismatch.

---

[17] See, for example, Thompson (1972), Lounsbury (1978), Aveni (2001).

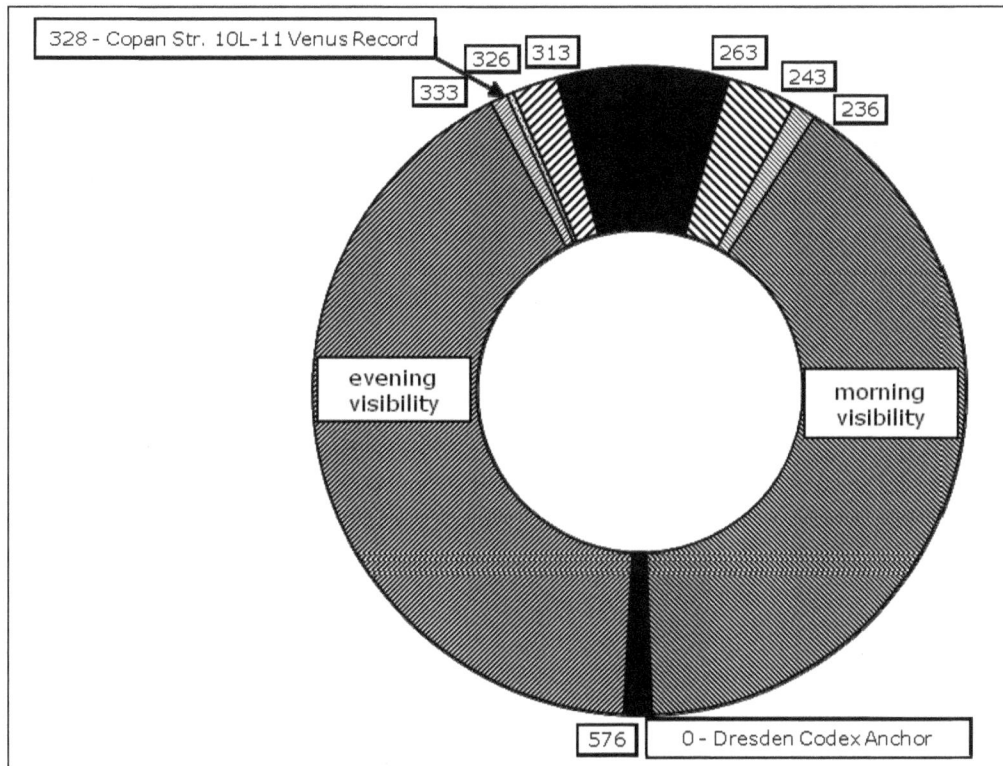

Figure 19: Copan Venus record relative to the Dresden Codex Page 24 anchor

So a straightforward reading of Page 24 of the Dresden Codex leading to an hypothesis of 9.9.9.16.0 1 Ajaw 18 K'ayab as an historical first morning appearance suggests an historical continuity between the Venus record of the Late Classic at Copan and one from the early Postclassic in the Dresden manuscript. While provocative, this continuity is, according to the literature, quite *un*expected. That is, the Venus Table anchor has had one very consistent interpretation over the last fifty years, and that has been one based on *dis*-continuity.

Virtually every scholar working on the Dresden Codex Venus Table since John Teeple has adopted (some version of) the following logic (Bricker and Bricker 2007:98-106):

1. recognition that the Venus Table's Long Count anchor is 9.9.9.16.0 1 Ajaw 18 K'ayab as recorded in the Preface (p. 24);

2. observation that the GMT places 9.9.9.16.0 1 Ajaw 18 K'ayab at a significant temporal distance from a first morning event;

3. because the GMT prediction does not place this anchor on or near an heliacal rise event, *assumption* that this anchor did not reflect an historical observation, but that it was mathematically contrived as an anchor to the table;

4. usage of the Preface to combine (both explicit and implicit) correction intervals with arbitrary numbers of uncorrected intervals in a best-fit approach to shift predictions to match observation over time;

5. argument that the best fit between the application of corrections within the Preface and computationally reconstructed visibilities of Venus provides the period during which the table was in use;

6. consideration of the accurate predictions of this table—after correction—to be support for or validation of the GMT calendar correlation on a day-for-day basis.

It should be clear from this overview that the GMT (Goodman-Martinez-Thompson) calendar correlation is intimately tied to the interpretations of the Venus Table over the last fifty years.[18] Yet we have just seen that the Copan record explicitly challenges the assumption of Point 2, which is dependent on the GMT's accuracy.

Resolving this conflict—or at least taking it seriously—we are led to a solution to perhaps the most enigmatic component of the Venus Table: the intent of the interval 1.5.5.0.

The assumption within Point 2 is not without justification. Aveni, for example, refers to Lounsbury's work on the interpretation of the 9.9.9.16.0 base date (2001:190-191). Lounsbury demonstrated that the interval between this date and the Ring Number in the Preface possesses unique characteristics. He recognized that the 9.9.16.0.0 interval, written explicitly between 6.2.0 and 9.9.9.16.0, comprised whole number multiples of 260, 365, 584, 780, 2,920, 18,980, and 37,960—and so

---

[18] A significant application to day-for-day conversions, however, does not seem to have been adopted until Michael Coe's publication concerning the work of Floyd Lounsbury (Aldana 2010).

constituted a "supernumber" (1978:787; Aveni 2001: 191). Based on this observation, and on the recognition of similarly composed intervals at Palenque, which connected historical to mythological times, Lounsbury suggested that Mayan scribes were intentionally contriving these dates for numerological purposes, *and not* for purposes of historical accuracy (1976:215). The upshot is that if the anchor in the Preface were contrived for numerological reasons, we should not expect that it would accurately predict historical astronomical phenomena (Aveni 2001:191; Bricker and Bricker 2007:100). That in mind, scholars have been free to assume that this contrived base date was not historically accurate, and so made allowance for the potential validity of the GMT.

On the other hand, it is not hard to recognize that the application of the GMT to the Venus Table as reviewed above is tautological: the GMT is assumed to be correct; then an arbitrary (i.e. a priori unspecified) number of intervals is used to bring the Venus Table's predictions into line with GMT-produced historically observable events; and then the result is considered corroboration that the GMT is correct.[19] For the most part, though, scholars have not been concerned with this; instead they have focused on the technical processes of correction (Bricker and Bricker 2007; Lounsbury 1992a, 1992b; Paxton 2001:76).

We will not dwell on the nuances of the issue here. For one, GMT-generated dates are rife within the published literature such that any challenge to it generally raises the hackles of contemporary Mayanists.[20] My own assessment, though, is that resistance to challenges generally derives from a lack of attention to the details of the GMT argument. That is, a challenge need not be dramatic if a specific clarification is kept in mind: the aspect of the GMT that ties the Long Count to the Gregorian/Julian calendars *on a daily basis* relies only on the Venus Table and an assumption of calendric continuity from the Early Classic through twentieth-century highland Mayan day-keeping practices. That is, while few are prepared to contest the general acceptability of the GMT to within the tolerances of C-14, thermoluminescence, or obsidian hydration dating techniques (and such a challenge is not proposed here), the point is that challenging the day-for-day claims of the GMT would impact none of these.

Further resistance to GMT challenges also often make reflexive appeal to the ethnohistoric record. These appeals, however, mask an extremely complex string of arguments leaping from one context to the next. An excellent parallel example comes from the work of John Justeson and David Tavarez on calendric records within a series of booklets from the mid-colonial period in Oaxaca and the complexity of recovering a clear continuity among dates recorded within a relatively small geographic region (2007; see also Aldana 2008). So as not to muddy the waters with a colonial Zapotec data set, however, we have only to go back to Thompson to get a taste of what is involved.

Thompson reviewed part of the argument for a continuous Calendar Round in Appendix II of *Maya Hieroglyphic Writing* (1960). There, he begins with the four records that give the surrender of Cuauhtemoc as 1 Coatl corresponding to August 23, 1521, which synchronize with the counts of twentieth-century Guatemalan daykeepers (1960:303). Certainly, that would appear to be impressive evidence behind a continuity hypothesis. On the other hand, these dates on either end are non-synchronous with an intermediate Mayan date: Diego de Landa's assignment of 12 Kan 1 Pop to July 26, 1553. According to the Aztec-modern-Mayan count, Landa's date is off by one day. Thompson explains away the discontinuity by suggesting that Landa had simply misinterpreted his data as he wrote it up for publication (1960:304).

While we might be persuaded by two secure data points and one massaged data point supporting a continuous count over 500 years and reaching from the Aztec capital to the Mayan highlands, there are, of course, other complications. These are far too messy, though, to cover with anything approaching persuasion without a much fuller treatment. That fuller treatment has been deferred to another manuscript entirely (Aldana 2010).[21]

Besides the complicating data from other ethnohistoric sources, there are other issues that come from a closer look at the factors influencing arguments for continuity. For one, a continuity between Aztec and Postclassic Mayan Calendar Rounds is of itself interesting, but it may not be as compelling as it at first appears. Synchronous calendars with the Aztec may have been convenient but also may have been imposed. Either situation leaves open the possibility that the counts were non-synchronous before contact with the Aztec Empire.

The point of this brief digression is simply to demonstrate that the ethnohistoric data is far from overwhelmingly in support of an argument for continuity—it does not readily support an assumption of continuity on its own. Such a result resonates with Edward Calnek's recent argument that Calendar Rounds in use within the heart of the Aztec Empire may have been unsynchronized (2007). The point is simply that appeals to the ethnohistoric record are

---

[19] Floyd Lounsbury did recognize the less than desirable logical quality of this argument, but resorted to another argument to substantiate his case. Namely, Lounsbury appealed to the fact that Venus was in a rare conjunction on the date that he reconstructed as the anchor to the first correction of the table. Because of the rarity of the conjunction, Lounsbury suggested that it could not have been coincidence; rather it demonstrated intent. See also Aldana (2001, 2007).

[20] This may be too strong a statement "generally," but it is uncontestable within the archaeoastronomy community, particularly since much astronomical interpretation depends explicitly on the day-for-day validity of the GMT. Martin and Grube (2001) have gone so far as to give numerous events only in the GMT generated Christian correlated dates.

[21] This is perhaps the larger motivation for a day-for-day correlation, as it allows for explicit continuity between Classic Mayan dates, the records of Colonial period, and the modern practices of K'iche' day-keepers. Such continuity, while highly desirable, is only obtainable if we assume that a single correlation is correct, and that all dates that deviate from this correlation were written in error.

anything but straightforward, and they at least allow for us to entertain the possibility that the day-for-day accuracy of the GMT is not as secure as its popularity suggests.

In any case, the importance of the Copan record in this debate should now be obvious. Since it is reasonable to assume that its production was independent of the Dresden Codex records (or at least that the record pre-dated the Dresden Codex), the Copan date allows us to test the *hypothesis* that ancient Mayan astronomers considered the 9.9.9.16.0 date to have been fictitious. That is, if the Venus Table anchor was inaccurate in historical times because it was purely a computational fiction employed for astrological purposes, with no ties to observation, then we would expect an independently recorded Venus event to deviate substantially from its predictions. Instead, as we have seen above, the Copan record quite precisely follows the metric set by the 9.9.9.16.0 Dresden Codex Venus Table anchor.

This observation may seem relatively unimportant, but in fact, it should carry substantial weight. That is, if we take into consideration only the Dresden Codex, then, even though it is internally quite complex, it may be analogized to a situation in which we want to fit a curve through only a single data point. Any given interpretation of the Dresden Codex Venus pages still only yields a single data point. Until now, no other independent data points have been securely demonstrated from the Classic or Postclassic periods.[22] The record from Copan, however, constitutes an independent *second* data point. Recognized as a Venus record of significance, we are compelled to ensure that any given interpretation of Venus calendrics fits *both* the Dresden manuscript and the Copan inscription. Traditional interpretations of the Dresden Codex Venus Table, however, have ignored the Copan record.

Finally, it is worth stepping back to consider the implicit models here for long-term record-keeping practices. If, as suggested by the traditional approach to the Venus Table, it were common practice to include fictitious Venus records within an ephemeris without explicitly noting that they are fictitious, then this would limit the utility of the manuscript outside of its contemporary use. It also may imply that the work was done in one great feat. If, on the other hand, actual historical observations were included with predicted ones—as would be the result of the hypothesized reading of pages 46 – 50—then such accumulations of data could have been used over centuries to produce the kind of subtlety evidenced within the Dresden Codex Venus Table.

This review of the complications arising through the recognition of calendric continuity between the Dresden Codex and Copan raises one more concern. If the Copan record suggests that the Venus Table anchor was accurate in predicting a Venus station, what, then, do we make of Lounsbury's compelling evidence for contrivance?

Recently, I have shown that in all likelihood, Mayan calendric contrivance worked in a direction opposite to the one proposed by Lounsbury (Aldana 2007:108). Specifically, it is likely that *mythological* dates (for example here, the 1 Ajaw 18 K'ayab Ring Number assigned to 6.2.0) were under-constrained; in written or oral traditions they probably were anchored only by a 260-day count date or possibly a haab date. The task of the Mayan scribe would have been to reconstruct the mythological date using significant historical dates along with the procedures of contrivance (Aldana 2007:108, 113-122). Viewed in this way, the purpose of contrived numbers, then, were to numerologically "discover" relevant placements of these partial dates within mythological Long Count times.

A relatively straightforward example comes from Waxaklajun Ub'aah K'awiil's contemporary at Palenque, Ahkal Mo' Nahb. The latter's altar in Temple XIX records the ancient event of 'an axing' of a Cosmic Dragon (Aldana 2001:19-31, 2007; Velasquez 2005; Stuart 2005:68-77). This mythic event occurring on a 1 Etz'nab 6 Yaxk'in Calendar Round date certainly looks convenient since Etz'nab is iconographically represented by flint, and Yaxk'in translates to "New Day." But I have shown that it was also contrived to link this event with the protagonist's "birth date" and Ahkal Mo' Naab's taking of the altar ceremony using lunar periods (2007:185).

The relevance here, therefore, is that if contrivance worked in the Dresden Codex as it did at Palenque, the 9.9.9.16.0 1 Ajaw 18 K'ayab anchor might very well have been observationally derived and historically recorded, such that it was the Ring Number that was contrived.

The result of this exploration of the potential continuity between the Dresden Codex Venus Table and the Copan Venus record is, for one, that we confront the possibility of a very nice example of linguistic, thematic, and calendric continuity across the Postclassic/Classic divide. On the other hand, there is so much inertia behind the current interpretation of the Venus Table (including at least 50 years of scholarship), that this one example may be insufficient to have much impact. The story does not end here, though, since the hypothesis of seeing 9.9.9.16.0 1 Ajaw 18 K'ayab as a historical anchor turns out to be productive in another important way.

3.2 RE-READING PAGE 24

More important than the challenge to the GMT for this essay is that the continuity between the Copan inscriptions and the Dresden Codex anchor allows us to reconsider the actual use of the Preface. That is, there is no doubt that the Preface contains useful information for the placement of the Venus Table within Long Count historical time. Thompson made clear, though, that: "[a]ccording to the 11.16.0.0.0 [GMT] correlation

---

[22] See Aldana (2005) for the proposed "Star Wars" Venus records.

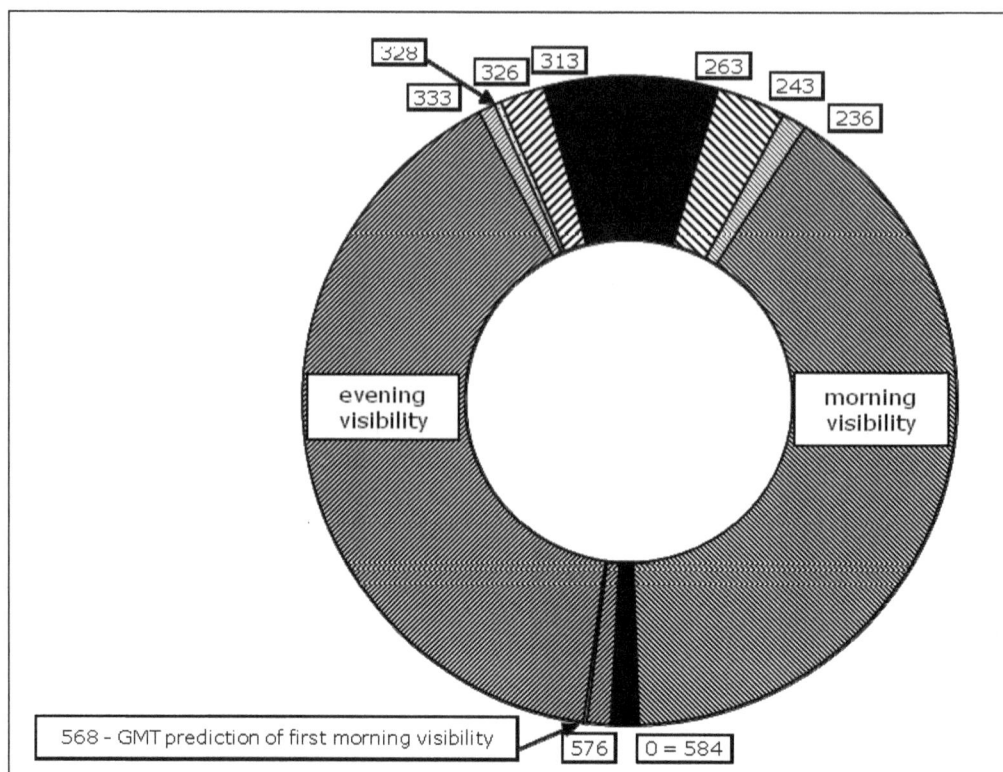

Figure 20: GMT predicted visibility for 9.9.9.16.0 1 Ajaw 18 K'ayab

heliacal rising of Venus after inferior conjunction should have occurred about 16 days after 9.9.9.16.0 1 Ahau 18 Kayab, the earliest base in the tables" (Thompson 1972:63). This problem is much worse than it might at first appear. Because Venus is only in inferior conjunction for approximately 8 days, an error of 16 days *later* would be a matter of concern, but not catastrophic—if one predicts that Venus will be morning star on a given date and it has been morning star for 16 days until that time, and will continue to be for another 250 days, that is significant. (See Figure 20) But that is not the case here. As the GMT predicts the phenomena, the 16 days go in the other direction so that the anchor to the Venus Table predicts a first *morning* visibility of Venus while it was still visible as *evening* star—and may have had 8 or more days of evening visibility left before it began inferior conjunction.

The traditional approach to resolving this discrepancy is impressive from a puzzle-solving perspective—though it certainly leaves something to be desired when it comes to the efficiency with which it handles the information explicitly recorded in the manuscript. To see this pattern, however, we must first take a closer look at the structure of the Preface.

Like Pages 46 – 50 of the Dresden Codex, Page 24 is broken in vertical halves. The left-hand side contains three columns of text, three numbers in Long Count positional format, and three Calendar Round dates. While enlightening in its own right, I forego treatment of the text here to focus instead on the dates and so mention only that two of the passages corroborate the importance

of the East as they both start off with *k'ahlaj lak'in* events.[23]

The first Long Count is a Ring Number—the equivalent of a negative integer, indicated by a knot tied around the value in the *k'in* position—6.2.0. This Ring Number is followed by the "zero date" of the Long Count, 4 Ajaw 8 Kumk'u, indicating that the scope of time addressed within these pages begins 6 haab and 40 k'in before 13.0.0.0.0 (i.e. on 12.19.13.16.0 1 Ajaw 18 K'ayab). Next, we have the aforementioned contrived interval of 9.9.16.0.0 (= 1,366,560 days = 36 Great Cycles = 72 Calendar Rounds), which as a Long Count date would bring us back to 4 Ajaw 18 Kumk'u. As a Distance Number, though, it takes us to the next Long Count and Calendar Round date recorded: (6.2.0 + 9.9.16.0.0 =) 9.9.9.16.0 1 Ajaw 18 K'ayab. (See Figures 2 & 3) Finally, the left-hand side of the page ends with the Calendar Round date of 1 Ajaw 18 Wo. We have seen some of the significance of the contrived numbers above; here we will find that the last two Calendar Round dates are related to the material on the right-hand-side of the Page 24.

The right-hand side of Page 24 comprises a table of intervals that (for the most part) make intuitive mathematical sense. The bottom section of the right-hand side contains the first four multiples of 2,920. (See Figures 2 & 3) This number, 2,920 (= 5 x 584), is the interval elapsed over one complete row of 260-day count

---

[23] For readings of this text, see Aldana (n.d.) or Schele and Grube (1997).

dates running across pages 46 – 50. Accordingly, the date at the end of the first row (column four, page 50) is 9 Ajaw, matching the date at the bottom right hand corner of Page 24 and corresponding to the application of 2,920 days to the base of 1 Ajaw. The next interval on Page 24 (third column, bottom row), 5,840 (= 2 x 2,920) is accompanied by 4 Ajaw, which is the final date of the second row of the Table (column 4, row 2, page 50). The bottom three sections of the table (of four intervals each) thus proceed along the steps mimicked by the rows in the Venus Table proper from 1 x 2,920 :: 9 Ajaw through 12 x 2,920 :: 6 Ajaw.

The next multiple, the thirteenth, brings us back to 1 Ajaw. It is not, however, the next interval in the progression. Instead, the thirteenth multiple of 2,920 shows up in the top section of the table. This top section records multiples one through four of 37,960 (= 13 x 2,920) and each is accompanied by a 1 Ajaw date, making clear that the base of the projection forward in time was also a 1 Ajaw date.[24] So overall, the table on the right-hand-side of Page 24 contains the multiples of 2,920 that mimic a progression down the rows of the Venus Table, and multiples of 37,960 that take one complete table forward to later complete tables. This much is straightforward. In this progression, though, we have skipped a section—one that while also preserving 1 Ajaw end dates, requires subtler interpretation.

It was Teeple, who showed that we may consider the numbers in this skipped section to be "correction intervals" since respectively, they preserve the 1 Ajaw portion of the date while shifting the haab companion (1931). The need for correction arises because the Table idealizes Venus Rounds to 584 days, whereas observationally, Venus's synodic period is 583.9214 days. Over a Great Cycle (104 haab), this 0.0786-day difference (~2 hours) accumulates to 5.1 days. (See Figure 21) Accordingly, Teeple proposed that the intervals in columns 1, 2, and 3, corresponded to corrections of 8, 12, and 8 days respectively. But Teeple also noticed a provocative pattern generated by an implicit interval. Subtracting the third correction interval from the second yields a new correction interval of 4 days (68,900 − 33,280 = 35,620). Applying this correction interval (35,620 days) to an anchor of 1 Ajaw 18 K'ayab produces a Calendar Round sequence of:

1 Ajaw 8 Yax

1 Ajaw 18 Wo

1 Ajaw 13 Mak

1 Ajaw 3 Xul.

Of these five dates, only 1 Ajaw 8 Yax does not show up in either the Preface or the Venus Table (Bricker and Bricker 2007:102). The implication, then, is that (if we ignore 1 Ajaw 8 Yax) this implicit correction interval may have been used to move from one explicitly recorded base date to another in order to make up for the discrepancy between prediction and observation over time. (See Figure 24) All scholars working on the Venus Table since him have followed suit (Bricker and Bricker 2007:98-104).

The overall procedure in the traditional interpretation, then, has been to add uncorrected intervals to the base date of 9.9.9.16.0 1 Ajaw 18 K'ayab until they make up the 16 days of error. That establishes the point at which the table matches observable events according to the GMT. From there forward, correction intervals are added to maintain proximity to hypothetical observation.

While Teeple's interpretation of the correction intervals makes mathematical sense, the methods scholars have proposed for making use of them are less than efficient. That is, there are four correction intervals recorded on Page 24 and four explicit Great Cycle multiples. Traditional methods use only one out of four of the explicit correction intervals and one "implied" interval. Of the Great Cycle multiples, only one of the four is used. (See Figure 23) Also, as we have seen, traditional methods do not use the recorded 1 Ajaw 18 K'ayab date as an accurate historical event; rather it becomes an artificial date to be corrected. This is not an impressively efficient use of the data explicitly recorded.

If we break with these assumptions, however, and instead accept 9.9.9.16.0 as an historical record of a first morning visibility event, then the resulting reading of the Preface is not only straightforward, but it makes simpler utilization of the correction and Great Cycle multiples recorded at the top of the right-hand side of the Preface.

The key here is following the connection between the Preface and the Venus Table itself. We have seen that adding whole number multiples of 37,960 to the base date Calendar Round of 1 Ajaw 18 K'ayab will bring us back to 1 Ajaw 18 K'ayab. So, progressions through the top section of intervals preserve the base Calendar Round date. Now, if we skip (momentarily) the rightmost correction interval of 1.5.5.0 (which has always been seen as a problem) and add the other three intervals to the base Calendar Round, we get:

1 Ajaw 18 K'ayab + 4.12.8.0 = 1 Ajaw 18 Wo

1 Ajaw 18 K'ayab + 9.11.7.0 = 1 Ajaw 13 Mak

1 Ajaw 18 K'ayab + 1.5.14.4.0 (+ 4.12.8.0) = 1 Ajaw 3 Xul

The results are precisely those Calendar Rounds generated by Teeple's approach—only here there is no superfluous 1 Ajaw 8 Yax, nor the implication of further unrecorded Calendar Rounds. Each of the resulting Calendar Round dates plays a well-known role within the Venus Table (See Figures 2a & 3a; 2f & 3f):

---

[24] There is significant erosion at the top of the page, but what is clearly discernable is a pattern strongly suggesting the reconstruction presented here and accepted by all scholars working on the pages. A strict sequence of four multiples of 65 Venus Rounds would be 5.5.8.0, 10.10.16.0, 15.16.6.0, and 1.1.1.14.0, each taking a day 1 Ajaw to another day 1 Ajaw. Still recognizable at the top of Page 24 are: ... 1.14.0 1 Ajaw, .. 6.0 1 Ajaw, ... 16.0 1 Ajaw, and 7/8.0 1 [eroded Day Sign].

Observationally Based VR Variation

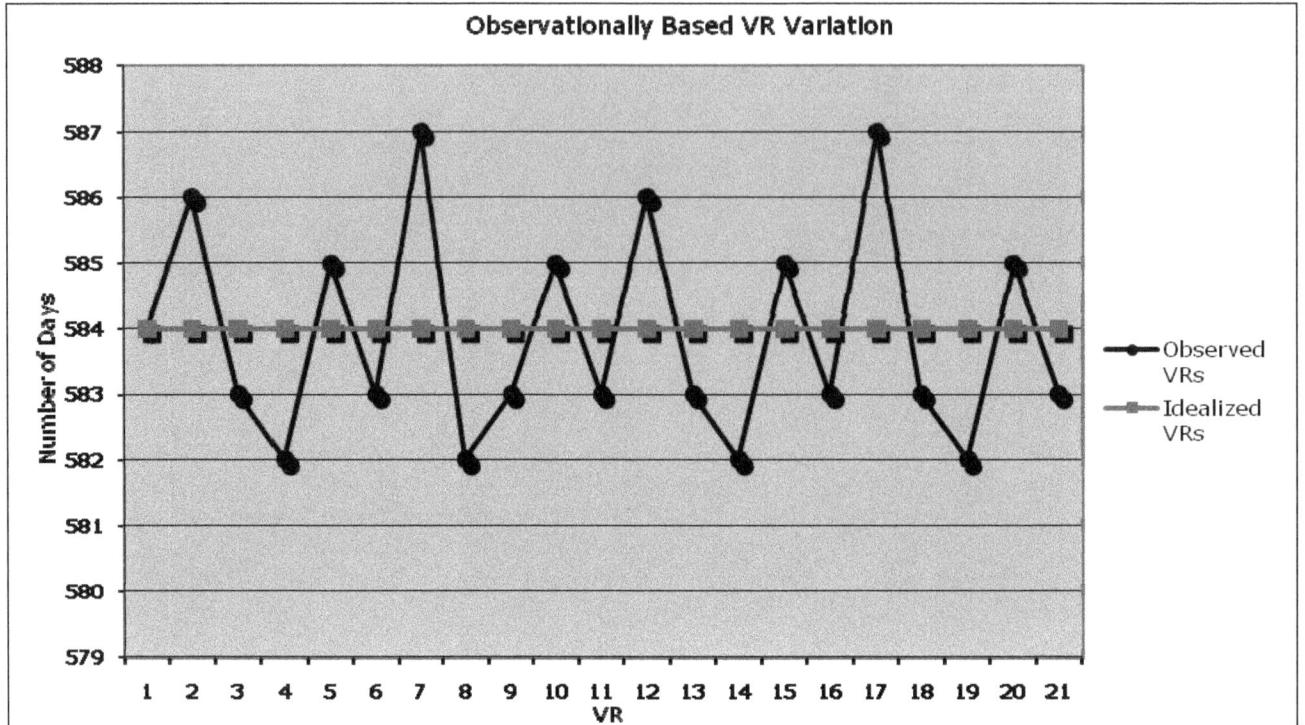

Figure 21 a) Venus's synodic period may vary by up to 4 days early or late on sequent cycles

Residual Error Accumulation

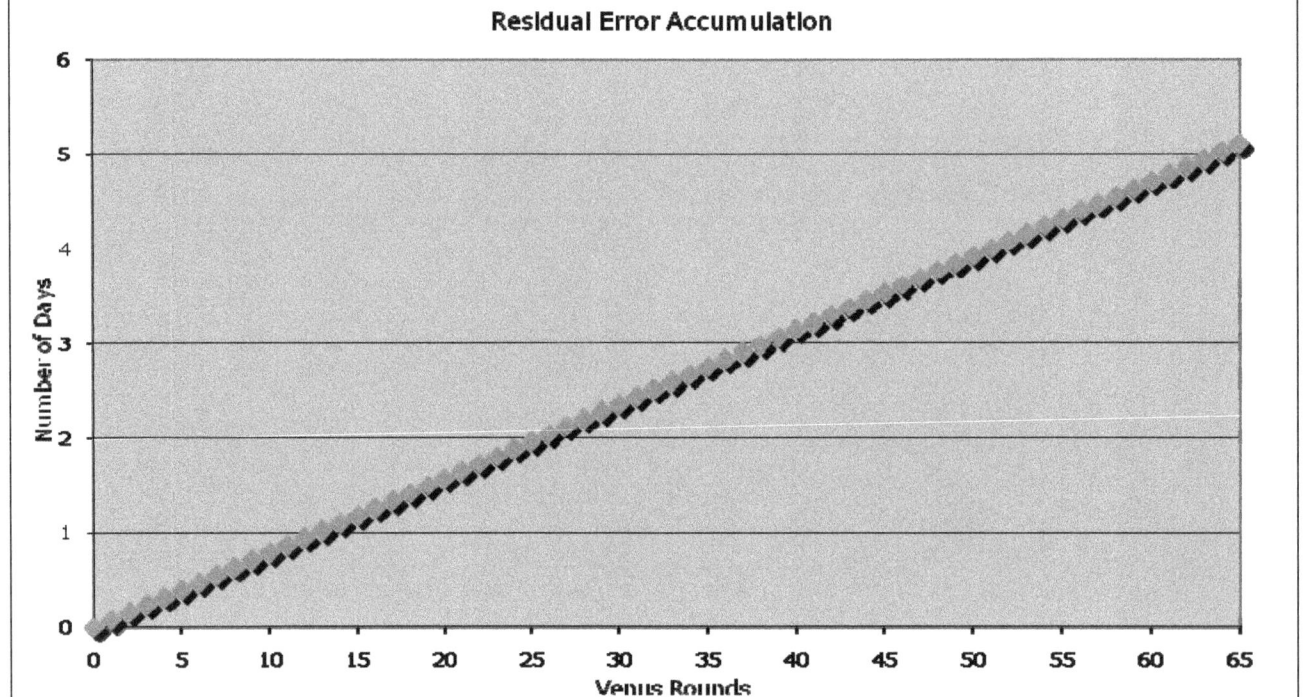

Figure 21 b) the observational error of any given synodic period must be distinguished from the error in determining the average synodic period—the latter generates a steadily growing residual error over time of 5.1 days over 104 years

1 Ajaw 18 Wo is the Calendar Round paired with the anchor (1 Ajaw 18 K'ayab) in the Preface.

1 Ajaw 13 Mak is the last Calendar Round in the first row of haab' dates on Page 50.

1 Ajaw 3 Xul is the last Calendar Round in the bottom row of haab' dates on Page 50.

In other words, avoiding Teeple's implicit correction interval and going straight to the intervals recorded in the Preface, we can reconstruct a progression that matches the one Teeple found (without the 'extra' one) and that matches what is recorded in the manuscript.

Such a reading makes good use of the correction intervals written explicitly in the Preface table, but the positions of these intervals in the table turn out to have utility as well: each correction interval is paired with the Great Cycle multiple it is meant to correct. That is, as noted, each uncorrected Great Cycle (37,960 days) adds 5.1 days

40

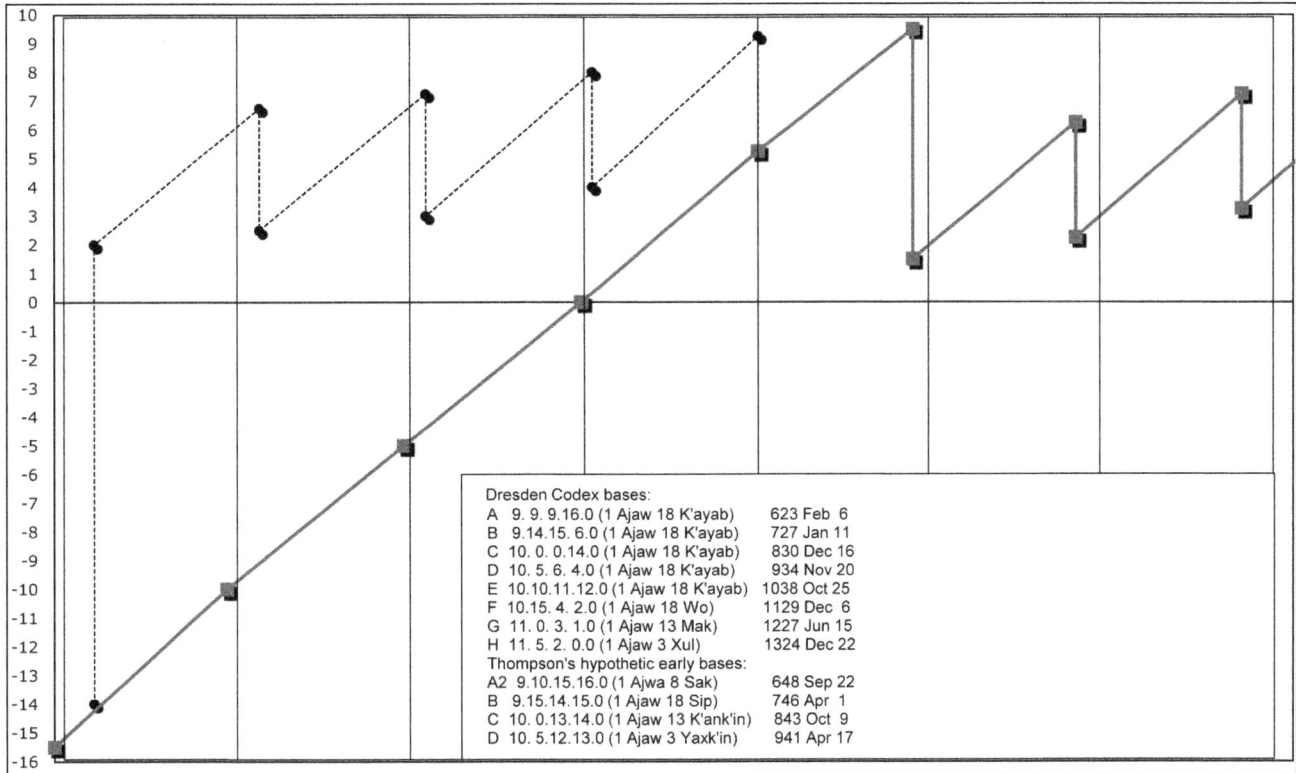

Figure 22: Reproduction of Lounsbury's (1983) graphic intercalation of Great Cycles and correction intervals

error between prediction and observation. The first correction interval (4.12.8.0) is located in the table precisely below the interval for two Great Cycles. (See Figures 2 & 3) Since the 4.12.8.0 correction interval provides a calendric adjustment of 8 days, two uncorrected rounds (10.2 days) would be balanced by one correction interval of 8 days.[25]

This pairing would be most efficient if the correction were not tacked on at the end of the Great Cycles. Rather, the system works best when one Great Cycle is added, then the correction is included to shift the base, and then the second Great cycle is the one that constitutes the table to be used. (See Figure 24) Hence, the first use of this system would have charted the dates starting at (9.9.9.16.0 + 5.5.8.0 + 4.12.8.0 =) 9.19.7.14.0 1 Ajaw 18 Wo, and running through one Great Cycle to end on 10.4.13.4.0 1 Ajaw 18 Wo. This would yield a revised Great Cycle beginning with a correction of -3 days, and completing that Great Cycle with an error of +2 days.

For the next correction, the scribe would go back to 9.9.9.16.0. Now s/he would apply the 9.11.7.0 correction interval (-12) to 3 uncorrected Great Cycles (+15) to begin and end on a Calendar Round of 1 Ajaw 13 Mak.[26]

Again, the interval for 3 uncorrected Great Cycles (15.16.6.0) is immediately above the 9.11.7.0 correction interval in the Preface. (See Figures 2a & 3a) Here, then, the base shifts such that the table would have started at (9.9.9.16.0 + (2 x 5.5.8.0) + 9.11.7.0 =) 10.9.12.3.0 1 Ajaw 13 Mak with an error of -2 days and ended on 10.14.17.11.0 1 Ajaw 13 Mak with an error of + 3 days.

Now, the top left entry in the table is a bit more complex with good reason. Whereas the second and third columns comprise intervals of 200 years and 400 years, the correction in the first column is huge: 4 Great Cycles yield 400 years, and the correction interval is even larger, at around 500 years, combining for a revision over a 900-year period. (For an anchor in the seventh century, that puts these predictions somewhere near the time of Contact.) Interestingly, though, the explicit correction interval only provides an 8-day compensation when 4 Great Cycles alone clearly require 20 days of adjustment.

Two factors, then, determine the procedure for this final adjustment. The first is that if we follow the other corrections, our adjustment should fall a bit short of the total error generated. Of the other two correction intervals, a serial application of 9.11.7.0 would balance the total error perfectly: 1.5.14.4.0 (-8) + 9.11.7.0 (-12); whereas the other leaves the adjustment short: 1.5.14.4.0 (-8) + 4.12.8.0 (-8). So, taking the second option, we encounter the second factor arguing for it: 9.9.9.16.0 + (3 x 5.5.8.0) + 1.5.14.4.0 + 4.12.8.0 = 11.15.12.16.0 1 Ajaw 3 Xul. That is, this set of paired adjustments (1.5.14.4.0 and 4.12.8.0) leads to the final base of the Dresden Codex Venus Table. (See Figure 23)

---

[25] The "match" between 8 and 10 days is actually better since the truncated interval must be inserted before the last uncorrected Great Cycle. Since the full 10 days of error are not generated until the end of this second Great Cycle, the start of the table of dates to be constructed should require an adjustment of 8 days. See further discussion below.

[26] The reader should note that here again, the 'correction' is just less than the accumulated error. This too suggests that the start of the new table should be at Correction + (n-1)*Great Cycles, where n is the number of Great Cycles in the top row affiliated with the stated correction.

Thompson applies this whole multiple of one complete table (**1.1.1.5.14.0** = 4 x 5.5.8.0) to the base date of 9.9.9.16.0 1 Ajaw 18 K'ayab to arrive at 10.10.11.12.0 1 Ajaw 18 K'ayab.

Thompson then applies the first correction interval **4.12.8.0** to arrive at 10.15.4.2.0 1 Ajaw 18 Wo.

Thompson's final move is to use the implicit interval (**9.11.7.0** – **4.12.8.0** = 4.18.17.0) to then maintain proximity to observation at 11.0.3.1.0 1 Ajaw 13 Mak and then 11.5.2.0.0 1 Ajaw 3 Xul.

a

Lounsbury applies this whole multiple of one complete table (**15.16.6.0** = 3 x 5.5.8.0) to the base date of 9.9.9.16.0 1 Ajaw 18 K'ayab to arrive at 10.5.6.4.0 1 Ajaw 18 K'ayab.

Lounsbury then applies one complete table (**5.5.8.0**) to arrive at 10.10.11.12.0 1 Ajaw 18 K'ayab, equivalent to Thompson's start date.

Lounsbury then applies the first correction interval **4.12.8.0** to arrive at 10.15.4.2.0 1 Ajaw 18 Wo.

Lounsbury's final move is to follow Thompson and use the implicit interval (**9.11.7.0** – **4.12.8.0** = 4.18.17.0) to then maintain proximity to observation at 11.0.3.1.0 1 Ajaw 13 Mak and then 11.5.2.0.0 1 Ajaw 3 Xul.

b

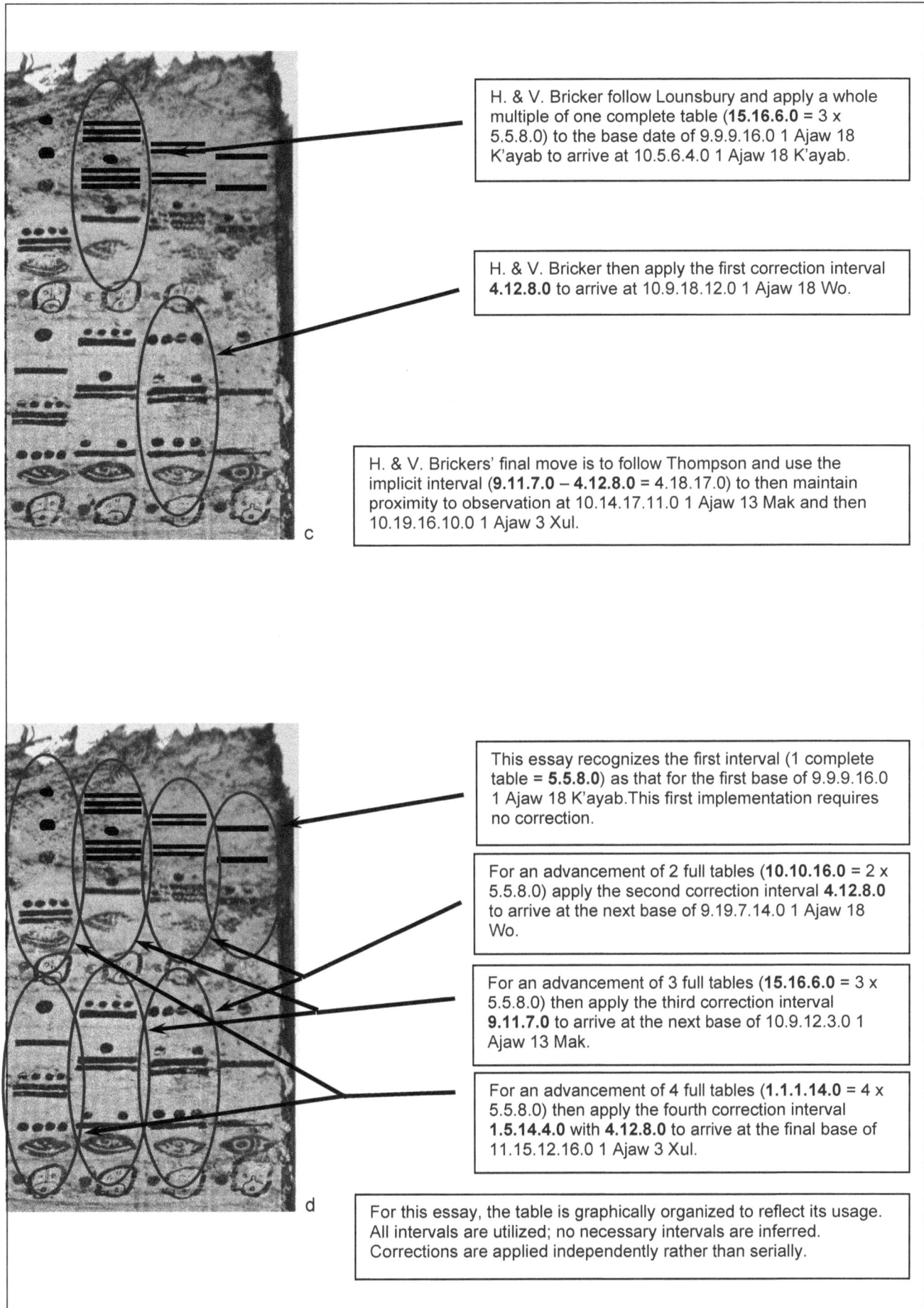

H. & V. Bricker follow Lounsbury and apply a whole multiple of one complete table (**15.16.6.0** = 3 x 5.5.8.0) to the base date of 9.9.9.16.0 1 Ajaw 18 K'ayab to arrive at 10.5.6.4.0 1 Ajaw 18 K'ayab.

H. & V. Bricker then apply the first correction interval **4.12.8.0** to arrive at 10.9.18.12.0 1 Ajaw 18 Wo.

H. & V. Brickers' final move is to follow Thompson and use the implicit interval (**9.11.7.0 – 4.12.8.0** = 4.18.17.0) to then maintain proximity to observation at 10.14.17.11.0 1 Ajaw 13 Mak and then 10.19.16.10.0 1 Ajaw 3 Xul.

c

This essay recognizes the first interval (1 complete table = **5.5.8.0**) as that for the first base of 9.9.9.16.0 1 Ajaw 18 K'ayab. This first implementation requires no correction.

For an advancement of 2 full tables (**10.10.16.0** = 2 x 5.5.8.0) apply the second correction interval **4.12.8.0** to arrive at the next base of 9.19.7.14.0 1 Ajaw 18 Wo.

For an advancement of 3 full tables (**15.16.6.0** = 3 x 5.5.8.0) then apply the third correction interval **9.11.7.0** to arrive at the next base of 10.9.12.3.0 1 Ajaw 13 Mak.

For an advancement of 4 full tables (**1.1.1.14.0** = 4 x 5.5.8.0) then apply the fourth correction interval **1.5.14.4.0** with **4.12.8.0** to arrive at the final base of 11.15.12.16.0 1 Ajaw 3 Xul.

d

For this essay, the table is graphically organized to reflect its usage. All intervals are utilized; no necessary intervals are inferred. Corrections are applied independently rather than serially.

Figure 23: Approaches to reading the correction intervals on Page 24 of the Dresden Codex Venus Table:
a) Thompson's method; b) Lounsbury's method; c) Bricker and Bricker's method; d) the method proposed here

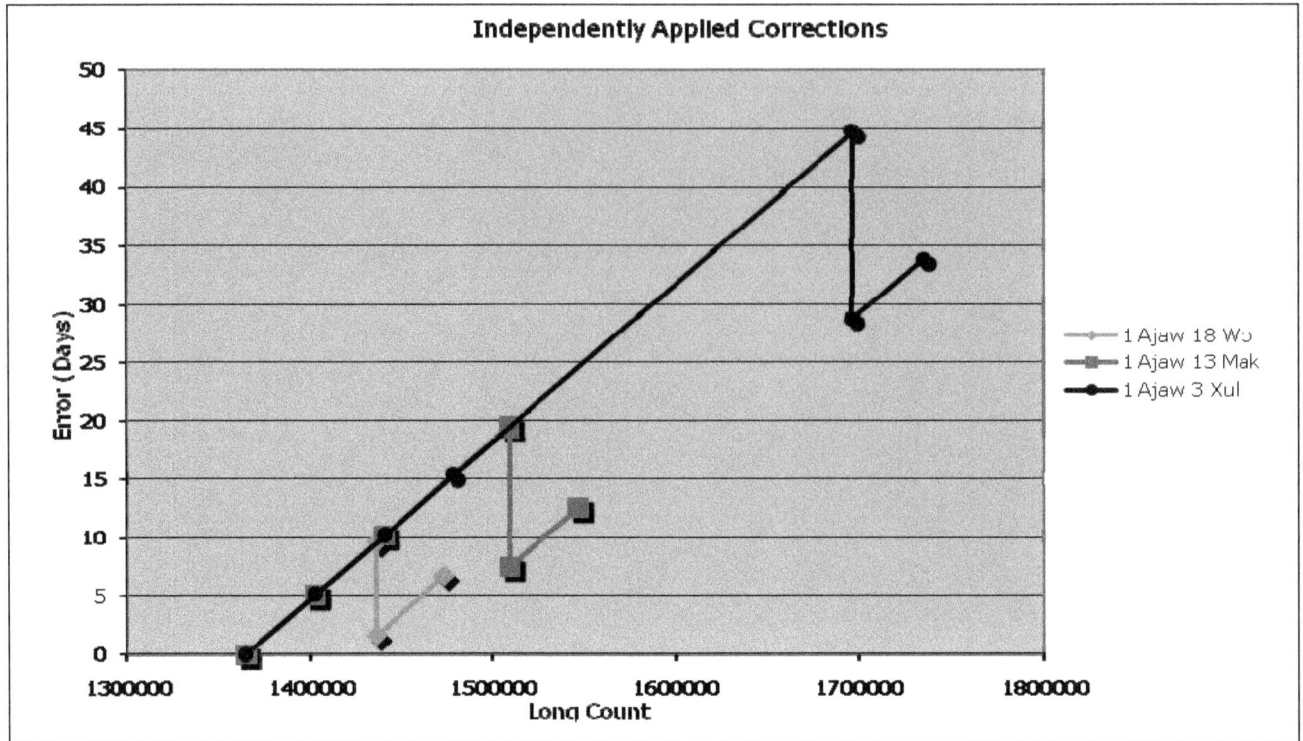

Figure 24: Graphic intercalation of Great Cycles and correction intervals according to the revision proposed here

Like Teeple's reading, then, this interpretation recovers the three Calendar Round anchors of the Venus Table using the intervals in the Preface. This reading, though, has the advantages over Teeple (and his followers) that we do not have to infer correction intervals, and we have no arbitrarity concerning which correction applies to which Great Cycle multiple.

In taking this approach, however, another difference arises. That is, whereas current approaches tack one correction onto the next serially, under this reading, each correction requires a return to the base such that the top two sections of the Preface pair uncorrected Great Cycles with the correction intervals necessary to balance out the accumulated error.

The proposed new reading then has its advantages in the efficiency with which it utilizes the numbers explicitly recorded. But one of the biggest factors behind the strength of the Teeple-derivative interpretations is the accuracy of the predictions generated. Indeed, we saw at the beginning of this essay that one of the key characterizations of the Venus Table referred to its accuracy in the long term. Any new proposal for reading the Preface, then, requires some consideration as to how accurate its shifts would have been. In particular, since this approach assumes that the 9.9.9.16.0 base date was tied to historical observation, then the visibilities of Venus after correction should also reflect a reasonable association to reconstructable historical observation. In other words, this model assumes that 9.9.9.16.0 was recorded as an actual Venus first morning visibility event. If we presume that the table of 260-day count dates corresponded to the 13 Mak anchor and that therefore the Codex was in use

during this time, then this means that the first correction—that shifting the haab date to 18 Wo—was also historical. If so, then the base date of 1 Ajaw 18 Wo should also have corresponded to a first morning visibility with sufficient accuracy to warrant the next projection.

Since we no longer have the convenience of an established calendar correlation, we cannot simply check the computer-ephemeris-generated historical visibilities of these dates. On the other hand, we can take the average synodic period of Venus, as it has been astronomically determined, and check the dates relative to this.[27] Doing so, we find that the difference between 9.9.9.16.0 and the anchor of the 1 Ajaw 18 Wo table at 9.19.7.14.0 (an interval of 200 years) corresponds to an observable difference of only 1.5 days (9.19.7.14.0 – 9.9.9.16.0 = 9.17.16.0 = 71,240 days = 122.0027 synodic Venus periods = 122 synodic periods and 1.5 days). Clearly, this first correction would have been perfectly operable given the observational tolerances of Venus visibilities and so would have warranted another projection. (See Figure 21a)

By the same protocol, the position within the synodic period of Venus on the next shift, corresponding to 10.9.12.3.0 1 Ajaw 13 Mak would have differed from the position on 9.9.9.16.0 by 7 days (10.9.12.3.0 – 9.9.9.16.0 = 1.0.2.5.0 = 144,820 days = 248 Venus Rounds and 7.5

---

[27] Taking this approach requires some caution. In particular, the periods of the planets are known to change with time. While this is trivial for most purposes, the dates in the Venus table are separated by hundreds of years. Such intervals bring into play differences of hundredths of a day in terms of accuracy. Nevertheless, given this caveat, we should be able to proceed by allowing some temporal tolerance.

days). This may have strained the limits of observational tolerance, but it still would have been operable, qualified of course by the specific manner in which the Venus Table was used.

The final shift to 11.15.12.16.0 1 Ajaw 3 Xul would have deviated by almost 29 days. Clearly such a table would have deviated too significantly to be of predictive use. On the other hand, if the 1 Ajaw 13 Mak base corresponded to the period of use, then this final projection would have been constructed for consultation over 500 years in the future. While not reflecting the accuracy claimed by Thompson, 29 days over 332,280 days is an error of less than 0.01%--impressive by any reckoning.

Now, since the utility of this correction would have been over 900 years after the base date, and in order to see the more likely rationale for the last correction, we must address an often-ignored element of the Preface.

3.1 *1.5.5.0*

Up to this point, we have ignored the anomalous interval within the Preface table. In fact, this is almost unremarkable since most treatments of the Dresden Codex either skip this interval entirely (Bricker and Bricker 2007; Paxton 2001), or comment on its enigma (Aveni 2004:186). Here we will find that, once again, if we leave behind the GMT and follow the logic of the mathematics within the manuscript, a solution presents itself.

The issue here is that the first element of the row of corrections appears completely out of line with the other three. Eric Thompson argued that the number itself was a mistake—probably a copyist's error (1972:63). He suggested that the 1.5.5.0 (= 9,100) interval recorded in the table should have been 1.6.0.0 (= 9,360), allowing for a still unorthodox, but slightly more useful, correction of +16 days. Floyd Lounsbury (1992b), on the other hand, took the number as written seriously. His key insight, which we take up here, is that the interval 1.5.5.0 embodies the same mathematical form as the others—the only difference, he proposed, was one of scale.

Lounsbury recognized that each recorded correction interval follows a coupling of Great Cycles to smaller correction intervals of 2,340 days (1992b:207). The smaller intervals take advantage of the facts that 2,340 = 4 x 585 + 4 and 2,340 mod 260 = 0. That is, subtracting these smaller intervals from Great Cycles mathematically preserves the 1 Ajaw ch'ol qiij date, yet compensates for the error between an idealized Venus Round of 584 days and its 583.9214-day synodic period through a shift of four days. Lounsbury's genius was to recognize that each of the correction intervals on Page 24 was intentionally constructed to correspond to a Diophantine Equation[28] using Great Cycles and 2,340-day correction intervals, where (1992b:208):

$$4.12.8.0 = 1 \times 5.5.8.0 - 2 \times 6.9.0$$
$$(\text{or } 33{,}280 = 1(37960) - 2(2340)) \tag{1}$$

$$9.11.7.0 = 2 \times 5.5.8.0 - 3 \times 6.9.0$$
$$(\text{or } 68{,}900 = 2(37960) - 3(2340)) \tag{2}$$

$$1.5.14.4.0 = 5 \times 5.5.8.0 - 2 \times 6.9.0$$
$$(\text{or } 185{,}120 = 5(37960) - 2(2340)) \tag{3}$$

even the aberrant interval:

$$1.5.5.0 = 4 \times 5.5.8.0 - 61 \times 6.9.0$$
$$(\text{or } 9{,}100 = 4(37960) - 61(2340)), \tag{4}$$

where the coefficient of 2,340 in each equation gives the number of 4-day corrections produced by the interval. Accordingly, we may immediately recognize the underlying structure to Teeple's 8-day corrections in Equations 1 and 3 and the 12-day correction in Equation 2.

By revealing the mathematical structure within these corrections, Lounsbury reduced the real oddity of the 1.5.5.0 interval from an anomalous number, to an anomalous implicit correction. As part of his signature approach, though, Lounsbury went further to investigate the steps that a scribe would have taken to generate a given result. What is really nice about this example is that if a scribe were to construct a set of corrections, they could have put together all of these intervals using the same method. More than that, the method is one that fits perfectly in line with what we understand about Mayan mathematics: these corrections use integer multiples of specific factors to generate whole number correction intervals.

On the other hand, this does leave us with the question of the utility of 61 4-day corrections (Equation 4). Lounsbury suggested that the interval's intent resided in its scope: a 244-day correction could only be useful for a very large accumulation of uncorrected Great Cycles (1992b:211). With this observation he returned to the argument for the GMT to suggest that the huge correction interval was used as a point of reference for the aberrant period of morning visibility (1992b:212-214). While he creates an interesting argument, if we (again) set aside the GMT-correlated portion of his argument, we confront an alternate internally consistent rationale for the 1.5.5.0 interval.

The logic of the Diophantine Equations above is compelling. Lounsbury proposed, however, that the utility of this correction came about with its anchor to the historical placement of the Venus Table, suggesting a very large interval of 40 Great Cycles between the contrived anchor of the Preface (-6.2.0), and the historical use of the manuscript (1992b:211). We have seen, though, that the size of the error is what drives the composition of the correction interval. If 1.5.5.0 calls for 244 days of correction, then it would make sense to determine how many Great Cycles are necessary to produce that kind of error. That is, each 2,340-day

---

[28] Lounsbury uses this terminology in his article (1992:208). A Diophantine Equation is one that takes the form $ax + by = c$ such that a, b, and c must be integers.

Table 6: Summary of the lower text on left-hand sides of Pages 46 – 50

Page 46	Page 47	Page 48	Page 49	Page 50
haab dates	haab dates	haab dates	haab dates	haab dates
deity	deity	*tsekya'n	*tsekya'n	*tsekya'n
*tsekya'n	Chak Ek'	deity	deity	deity
Chak Ek'	[N/A]	[N/A]	Chak Ek'	Chak Ek'
cosmic region	cosmic region	cosmic region	cosmic region	cosmic region
haab dates	haab dates	haab dates	haab dates	haab dates

interval introduces 4 days of correction, and each Great Cycle generates 5.1 days of error, thus

61 x 4 = 244 days of correction;

244 (corrected days)/5.1
(days needed to be corrected per GC) = 47.8 GCs

In words: it would take an interval of 47 (uncorrected) Great Cycles to generate 239.7 days of error. Thus, according to the logic of the mathematical language used to construct this interval, we should expect that the interval of 9,100 days was applied to an interval of (on the order of) 47 Great Cycles. But that leaves us with the question of where 47 Great Cycles might have come from.

Before addressing a possible source, there is one more line of reasoning that sheds light on all four problems: of 47 (or so) Great Cycles, of 1.5.5.0, of the method of returning to 9.9.9.16.0 for correcting the table, and of the baffling lower section of Pages 46 – 50. For the final consideration of the calendrics within the Venus pages, we return to potential linguistic evidence to support this newly proposed reading of the Preface.

The text in question resides in the bottom sections of Pages 46-50 between two rows of haab dates. (See Figures 2, 3 & 24) These rows end on Page 50 with two of the base dates noted: 18 K'ayab is the original anchor, and 3 Xul is the final shift produced by the longest correction. But the mediating text contains a different, as yet undeciphered, verb.

The verb's probable transcription is **tse/se-ya-ni**. Schele and Grube suggest the reading *tzeni*, which they translate as "feeds" so that, for example, the first column on Page 46 would read *"ulum tzeni Chak Ek' nah,"* or *'ulum* feeds *Chak Ek'* in the north' (1997:146-147). The reading of the Venus pages proposed here, though, raises a new possibility for consideration. Specifically, *-ya:n* plays the role of an inchoative suffix in Yucatec Mayan (Barrera Vasquez 1995:968).[29] If we take the first element as either an under-spelling or a logographic version of tsek, then here we have the verb *tse[k]ya:n* describing a Venus event and mediating between the 18 K'ayab and 3 Xul base dates. Also in Yucatec, *tsek* carries the meaning of

'prediction', or 'correction' ('sermón,' 'prédica,' 'castigo,' 'corrección' Barrera Vasquez 1995:856). The inchoative marker on the noun form of *tsek*, then, would suggest that the hieroglyphic text is explicitly instructing the reader that a correction is necessary between these two base dates.[30]

As far as our new interpretation of Page 24, this statement works nicely. That is, if this is explicitly noting a correction from 1 Ajaw 18 K'ayab to 1 Ajaw 3 Xul, then, it seems to be rejecting the hypothesis that corrections were applied serially as hypothesized by Teeple. Under this reading, the text tells us that each correction should begin with a return to the original base date of 1 Ajaw 18 K'ayab.

This still leaves unresolved the question concerning precisely what is being corrected. For this we recognize that unlike the *k'al* events of the text in the section above this one, the *tsekya'n* text varies in the order of its constituent glyphs. Nearly every page provides a different order for the glyphs between the haab dates—in two cases, even omitting a term. (See Table 6)

As has been long recognized, this lower section of text also introduces a column shift in both the deity names and the cosmic regions with which they are affiliated. Schele and Grube did not address it (1997), but we have seen that Aveni handled the shift by interpreting the narrative to fit the underlying astronomical phenomena (2001:194). I suggest instead that this text may be providing very specific instructions for the (distant) future use of the Venus Table.

That is, a really interesting pattern emerges when we notice that 46 Great Cycles—not 47[31]—added to the Ring Number base places us at (6.2.0 + 46 x 5.5.8.0 =) 12.2.4.6.0 1 Ajaw 18 K'ayab, the first complete Great Cycle after the completion of the twelfth baktun. This we may compare to the final corrected table—the one beginning on 11.15.12.16.0—which ended on 12.0.18.6.0 1 Ajaw 3 Xul. The difference between these two bases

---

[29] Whereas the Classic period inscriptions are heavily Ch'olti'an, Wald and Lacadena have shown Yucatecan creeping into the inscriptions of the Postclassic (2004.).

[30] Of course there are other semantic values that could be considered, but the core argument is that the correction value is productive in this context.

[31] The calculation leading to 47 Great Cycles was intended to determine the approximate scope of the computation. It was not intended to generate a specific number that would require strict adherence to be of value.

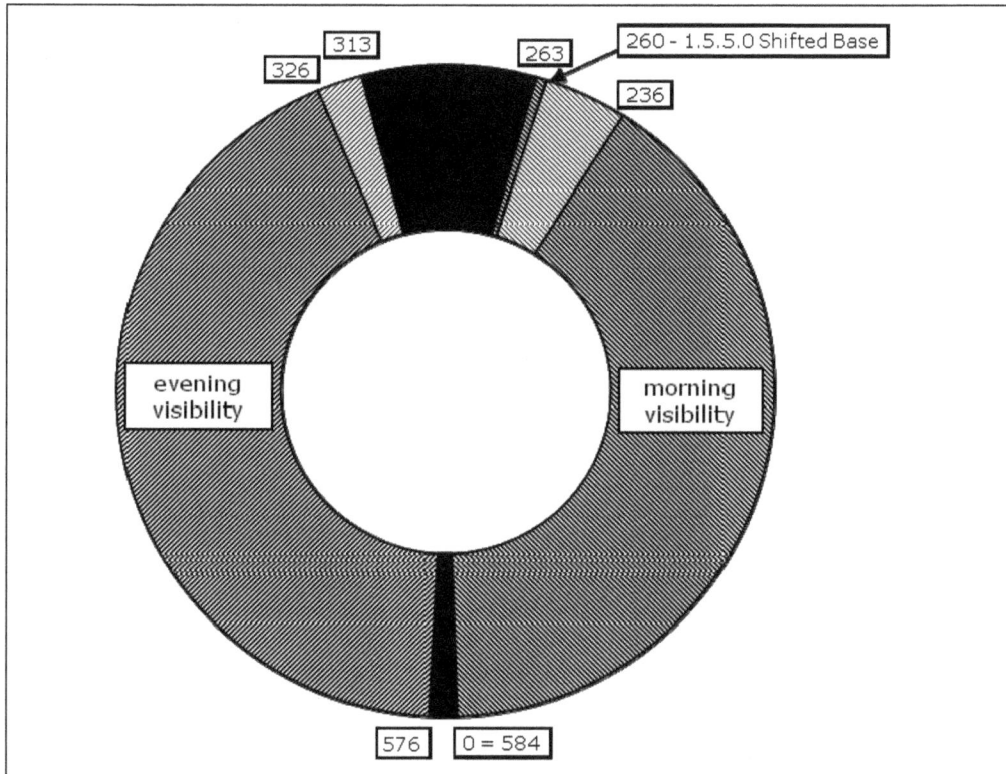

Figure 25: 260-day shift resulting in a move from first morning visibility to last morning visibility

(the end of the corrected 1 Ajaw 3 Xul table and the beginning of the next uncorrected 1 Ajaw 18 K'ayab table) is 1.6.0.0. The proximity of 1.6.0.0 and 1.5.5.0, separated by one 260-day count, is what led Thompson to believe that the latter was simply a copyist's error for the former (1972:63). Indeed, if 1.6.0.0 were intended, then we could see this as the connection of the last corrected Great Cycle of the twelfth baktun to the first uncorrected Great Cycle of the thirteenth baktun. Instead, a much more subtle resolution lies in the adherence to the recorded number.

Accepting the 1.5.5.0 interval and looking to Lounsbury's application of it (1992:211), we may subtract it from the later base:

$$12.2.4.6.0 - 1.5.5.0 = 12.0.19.1.0 \text{ 1 Ajaw 3 Wayeb (5a)}$$

so that:

$$12.0.19.1.0 - 13.0 = 12.0.18.6.0 \text{ 1 Ajaw 3 Xul.} \quad (5b)$$

That is, applying the 1.5.5.0 correction to the interval between 1 Ajaw 18 K'ayab and 1 Ajaw 3 Xul results in a gap of precisely 260 days. Rather than see this as a correction, the hieroglyphic text of Pages 46 – 50 suggest that this is intended to be *a shift*. That is, one thing that is not in dispute is that the *tsekya'n* phrase notes a shift forward through the cosmic rotation: North becomes East, West becomes North, South becomes West, and East becomes South. The rotation from South to East is shifted backward to correspond to the rotation from West to South. This would have the effect of rotating the

position of prominence from first morning appearance to *last* morning appearance. (See Figure 25)

This base shift—from first morning appearance to last morning appearance—is precisely the effect of changing the base date of the table from first morning appearance on 1 Ajaw 3 Xul to last morning appearance on 1 Ajaw 3 Wayeb. Since 1 Ajaw 3 Wayeb comes from the 1 Ajaw 18 K'ayab base date, we may hypothesize that this shift is what constitutes a correction from 1 Ajaw 18 K'ayab to 1 Ajaw 3 Xul—that which may be described by *tzekya'n* in the text.

The solution proposed here, therefore, is completely in line with Lounsbury's initial proposal: based on the Diophantine connection between this and all other intervals in the row, 1.5.5.0 should correspond to a very large correction—one moving from ancient (mythic) times into the future of the Postclassic scribes who recorded it. This solution also acknowledges Thompson's insight that 1.5.5.0 is only one chol qiij from 1.6.0.0. Here, though, we find that the discrepancy was not an error—it was intended to connect two future dates. In fact, 1.5.5.0 can be seen here as a type of 'completion' interval since it would bring together two lines of tracking Venus, tying together an historical trajectory to a shift based on an ancient anchor. Perhaps more importantly, this interpretation remains faithful to the text *as written*. No implicit intervals are inferred for their utility, and no intervals explicitly recorded are ignored.

While mathematically sound, this reconstruction raises the question of what may have caused the author of this

Figure 26: *Tse-ya-ni* in each column of the lower register of Page 48
within the Dresden Codex Venus Table

table to suggest a base shift so far into the future? We might speculate that it was being triggered by the end of the twelfth baktun, but that would require more evidence to substantiate.[32] Whatever the case, the current reading is the first to give a rationale for the 1.5.5.0 interval that is potentially substantiated by textual evidence from the Venus Table itself. And whether or not in the end this reading of *tse[k]ya:n* holds up to further scrutiny and the

accumulation of relevant data, the reading of the Venus pages proposed here is certainly more robust in utilizing the intervals, dates, and text actually written than previous approaches, which rely on implicit intervals, actively ignoring explicit intervals, and adhering to specious assumptions regarding the historical accuracy of recorded Long Count dates.

[32] It is suggestive that the Venus record at Copan preserves first evening appearance during the 10th baktun and that this shift would go from emphasis on first morning appearance in the 12th baktun to emphasis on last morning appearance during the 13th baktun. The pattern pretty strongly implies that last evening appearance would have been the focus during the 11th baktun, but this would all require much further study before becoming anything other than speculation.

Chapter 3:
K'AL IN ASTRONOMY, THE SECOND DOLL

To this point, we have problematized the "identity" of Venus in the Dresden Codex, unpacked the astronomy within Copan Structure 10L-11, and re-interpreted the reading of the Venus pages on a calendric level. All of this work has contributed toward a question of broader scope. In this chapter, we return to the issue that started it all, the verb *k'al*, in order to demonstrate that there is not only a rich context for *k'al* associated with royal ritual— there is also an astronomical context related to the Sun and Moon.

As mentioned above, the verb *k'al* can be found throughout the corpus in phrases involving white headbands (*sak huun*) and period endings (*k'altuun*). Perhaps as numerous as these references, **K'AL** can be found in the Lunar Series of Initial Series dates. In its most common form (as noted above relative to the Copan record), the Supplementary Series comprised the Cycle of Nine and the Lunar Series in the order of: Glyphs F, G, E, D, C, B, X, and A. Of the Lunar Series, the most straightforward part is the moon age, "Glyphs D and E" giving *X huliiy* – 'it was X [days ago]; it arrived.' The third component, comprising Glyphs X, B, and A give X_n *u k'aab'a 29*, or 'X_n is the name of the 29 [days].' Of primary import for this paper, though, is Glyph C. Note that in place of a stone, a white headband, or a 'celt,'[33] this **K'AL** hand holds the head of a lunar deity (Schele et al 1992; Linden 1991; Aldana 2006), and may be transcribed as **u-[#]-K'AL-[patron]-UH**. (See Figure 27)

From a computational perspective, Glyph C counts periods of up to six moons each, with each lunar deity governing (5 or) 6 moons before passing on duties to the next lunar deity (Schele et al 1992; Linden 1991; Aldana 2006; see also Teeple 1931). A straightforward implication here is that each *k'al* event corresponds to the completion of 29- or 30-day lunar cycles. Following Schele's and Grube's reading of the verb in the Dresden Codex, we might read this as the 'tying' of each lunar

deity's moon, with each deity collecting up to a maximum of 6 before passing duties on to the next deity.

Yet it is also valuable to highlight the fact that apart from a possible 'tying,' the *k'al* event is clearly associated with the completion of a time period. That is, the Lunar Series provides compelling evidence to go along with the Venus Table by using *k'al* to refer to the completion of (sub-) periods of larger cycles (i.e. each of six *k'al* events transpires before the next deity's *k'al* events begin).

In such case, we find that the completion of time periods works not only for Venus and the Moon, but for the Sun as well. In Yucatec, for example, we encounter the term *k'al k'in* "9: todo el dia 13ddp: todo el dia completo" (Barrera Vásquez 1995:370). A secondary definition, **K'ALAB K'IN**, helps with the analysis. According to Barrera Vasquez (1995:1), **-AB** is a verbal suffix, generating the passive form in the incompletive aspect. *K'alab* in modern Yucatec, therefore, plays the same role as *k'ahlaj* in Classic Ch'olti'an. Here, though, the absolutive of the verb is *k'in*, which is itself a bit ambiguous. Here, *k'in* could refer to the Sun; it could stand for day; or it could refer to time itself. The Yucatec definition of *k'alab k'in*, though, provides a solution: Barrera Vásquez gives "todo el dia completo" (1995:370). The referent, then, is the time period, day, and *k'alab* here is 'completing' in the sense of 'encompassing' it.

While these examples are "late," coming from the 19th century work of Juan Pío Pérez (1850) and work in the 1970s of Domingo Dzul Poot (and classified by Barrera Vásquez as "Maya Moderno"), there is significantly more time depth to the phrase. And when we look to the inscriptional contexts, we confront another continuity.

During the Terminal Classic period, a number of texts were carved into the walls of the structures at Chich'en Itza. These lacked the calligraphic flair of the inscriptions from earlier times, but their contents reveal unequivocal

---

[33] This celt is what Schele and Miller identified as *nen* 'mirror' (T614) (1983:20).

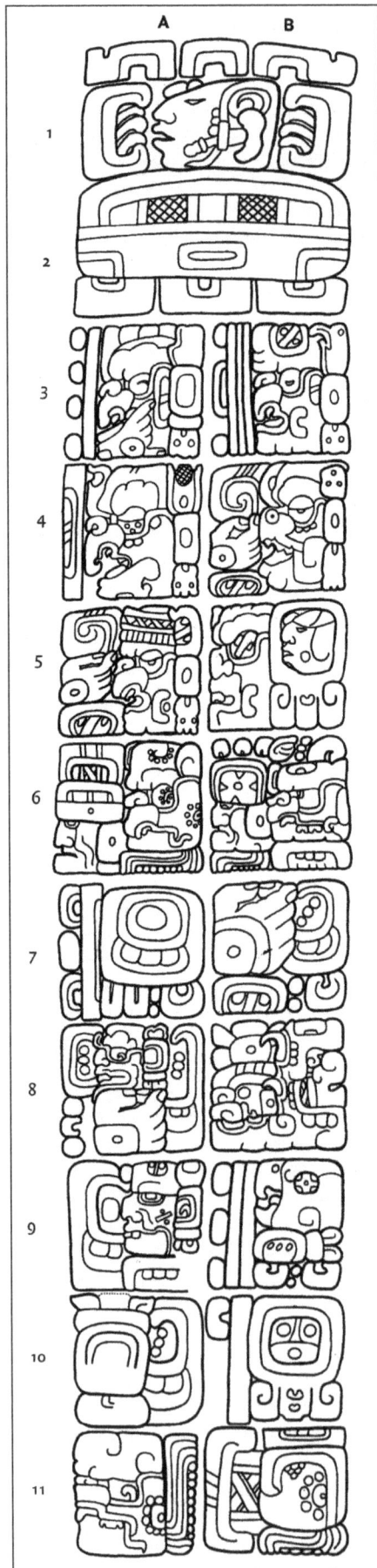

Figure 27: Glyph C of the Lunar Series on Qurigua Stela A at glyph block A8. (Drawing by Mathew Looper. Permission by M. Looper)

cultural continuity. For our purposes, we find a number of instances of the **K'AL** verb root, but here the iconographic element "held" is the sun. (See Figure 28) In line with the Yucatecan terminology, we may transcribe these as **K'AL-la-ja K'IN**, and read them as *k'ahlaj k'in*. Given its use on the Temple of the Four Lintels, *a-la?-ya k'ahlaj k'in tu/u-wojil yotot Yax Chit Jun Kan Ajaw Chanal K'uh*, we might be tempted to read this as "It took a whole day to carve these glyphs!" The controlling grammatical element here, however, is not *k'ahlaj k'in*, but the glyph preceding it *a-la?-ya*, which has unfortunately resisted clear interpretation, but seems to read "here; this (one)" (MacLeod and Polyukovych 2000; Boot 2005). Thus, we may instead translate the phrase as: "Here, the day is completed. It/this is the writing of the house of Yax Chit Jun Kan Ajaw, Celestial K'uh."

On the other hand, there is evidence that the period of time marked here is not simply that of a day, but that of a solar (sub-)period. When we look at all of the securely dated *k'ahlaj k'in* records from Chich'en Itza, we find that they fall on periods separable by standard portions of solar years (Aldana 2001:12). That is, the three secure dates are 10.2.9.1.9, 10.2.10.11.7, and 10.2.12.2.4. The first and last of these are separated from the second by one and a half years, whereas the first and last differ by 1095 days, or precisely three haab. In light of the practices of the Dresden Codex Venus Table and the Lunar Series, then, the straightforward inference is that theses *k'ahlaj k'in* events mark the completions of sub-periods of the solar year. If we allow for *k'in* to have this more general meaning, then we may have a more coherent reading of the phrase from the Temple of the Four Lintels inscription: "Here, the solar period is completed. It/this is the writing of the house of Yax Chit Jun Kan Ajaw, Celestial K'uh." In other words, a solar sub-period was commemorated at a temple that was owned by a celestial deity.

The point of this contextualization, though, is to suggest that 'tying' or 'binding' may be too specific as translations of *k'al*. A more abstract notion of 'completing,' or 'encompassing,' or even 'enclosing' would actually fit both the astronomical contexts and the royal ritual events.

This final step puts us in a position to consider the cosmological models connected to Mayan time, which is our final step toward an argument for resolution to last sentence.

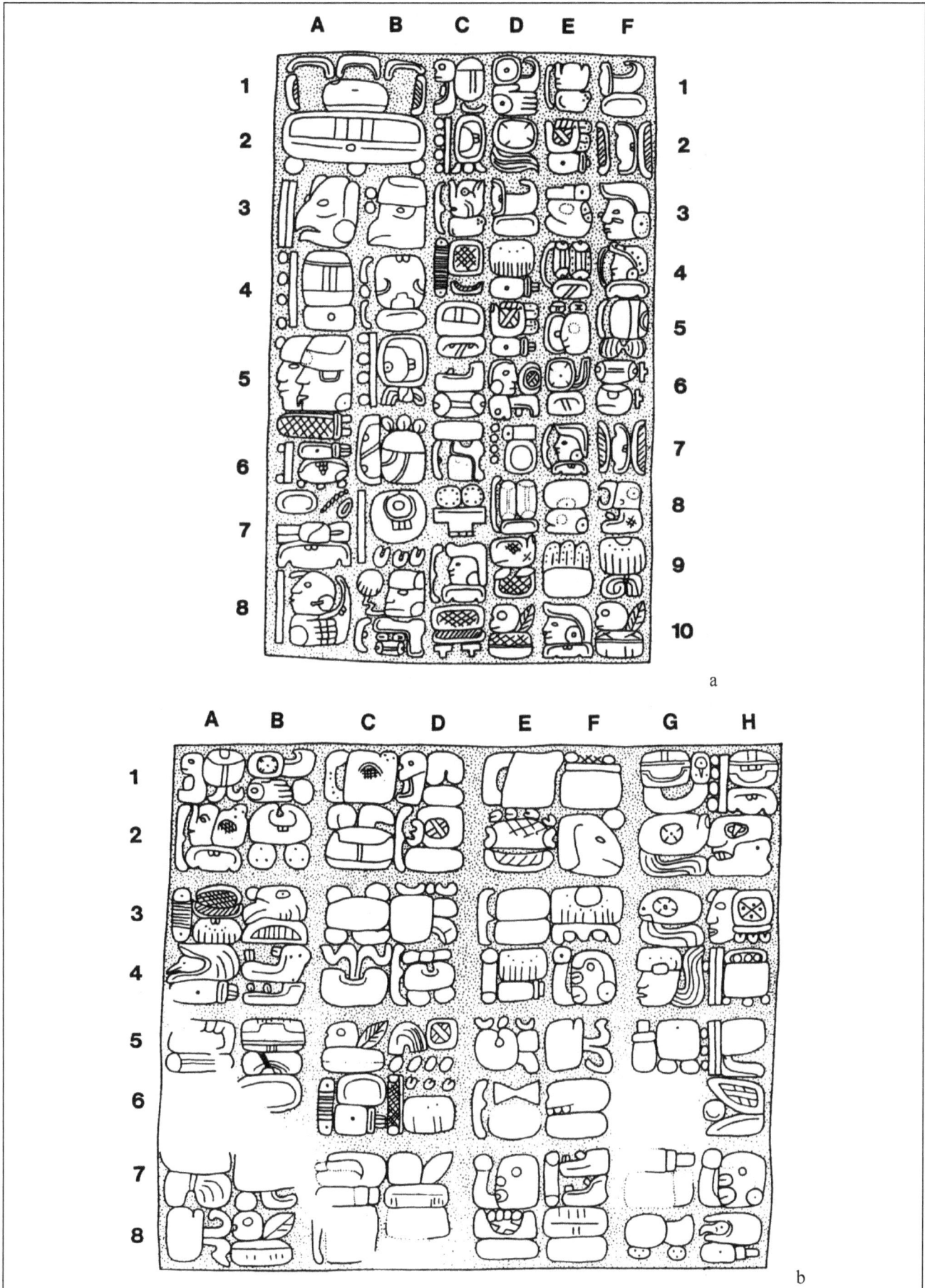

Figure 28: Yucatecan examples of *k'ahlaj k'in* at glyph block D1 in the Temple of the Initial Series Lintel 1 inscription at Chich'en Itza, and at B1 on Lintel 3 of the Temple of the Four Lintels, also at Chich'en Itza. (Drawing by Ruth Krochok)

Chapter 4:
K'AL IN COSMOLOGY, THE FIRST DOLL

Thus far, a close examination of the consensus interpretation of the Venus pages in the Dresden Codex has revealed a number of inconsistencies that have required reconsideration. I suggest that these are not merely loose threads to be tied up, but that they have provided access to a new paradigm for translating Mesoamerican calendric astronomy. The key lies precisely in an abstracted understanding of the term *k'al*. To see it, though, we must add to the above epigraphic, astronomic, and calendric considerations, an investigation into iconography. In doing so, we will heed Seler's advice concerning Central Mexican and Mayan cultures that "we have reason to expect that whatever progress shall be made in interpreting the documents of either of the peoples will be of use in throwing light upon the dark passages in the documents of the other of these two great civilized nations" (1904:391).

To begin this section on cosmology, we turn to a rather mundane activity: hunting. One of the definitions of *k'al* in Yuacatec noted above (Table 1) provides a very specific usage of the verb that sheds new light within the rest of its contexts. Specifically, in the Cordemex dictionary the full entry reads (1995:368):

> **K'AL** 3: armar lazos, ballestas 4: armar lazo 2. **K'ALAH** 3: V. **k'al** 3. **K'AL CHULUL** 2, 5:armar lazo para iguanas 4: k'al a chulul tu hol aktun: arma tu lazo en la boca de la madriguera 6: armar lazos a pájaros 8: vn armar el arco de la flecha, el lazo de la iguana 4. **K'AL K'AAN** 1: lazo que está armado ya; ti' biní u naabte u k'al k'aan: es ido a requerir sus lazos

From this definition, we find that there is a sense of 'arming weapons' that we also need to include in our understanding of *k'al*—that or we might conclude that these are simply homophonic terms of significantly different meaning. The specifics of the weapons, however, make it clear that we do not have to reach far for this to work. That is, each of these weapons is armed by forming a loop with a cord of some kind. The bow and the crossbow both are 'completed' by closing off an open loop with a cord. Arming these weapons constitutes tracing out a closed loop. But the third weapon is the most telling. *K'al chulul* is 'to arm a lasso-for-iguanas', i.e. a snare or trap. Better yet, the example sentence is very provocative. *K'al a chulul tu hol aktun* – 'arm your snare around the entrance of the burrow.' Arming here is very clearly forming a loop with a cord, 'circling' the entrance. The parallel between this phrase and the hiero-glyphic 'tying of headband' phrase is straightforward:

Table 7: Parallel sentence constructions based on *k'al*

Verb	Absolutive	Preposition	Possessed Object
k'al	*a chulul*	*t(i)*	*u hol aktun*
k'al	*sak huun*	*t(i)*	*u b'aah*

Under this comparison, *k'al* is not a <u>tying</u> of the white headband; *k'al* is the looping of the white headband around the ruler's head—the tracing out of a path around one's head and closing it off with a knot. Thus, the knot serves iconographically as a symbol for the closing of a loop—not for the process of tying. (See Figure 29) In fact, the same meaning is implied in the material utilized by Kaufmann. If we see the suffix *–b'al* in Ixil as an instrumentalizer,[34] we can read *k'alb'al* as 'that which traces a closed loop.' It is not hard, then, to recognize this as a perfectly functional description of a *cinturón*, which is its gloss by Kaufmann. The same argument holds for the *–b'il* suffix of Mam *k'alb'il*. (See Table 2) More importantly, the resulting reading of *k'al* as 'to trace out a closed loop' now becomes very productive relative to its other contexts, including those cosmological.

With this reading of *k'al*, we are able to make sense of the verb in three of its material contexts. First, *k'al* forms

---

[34] Michael Hughes states that *–bal* is productive as an instrumentalizer in Ixhil and probably Q'anjob'al (personal communication 2010).

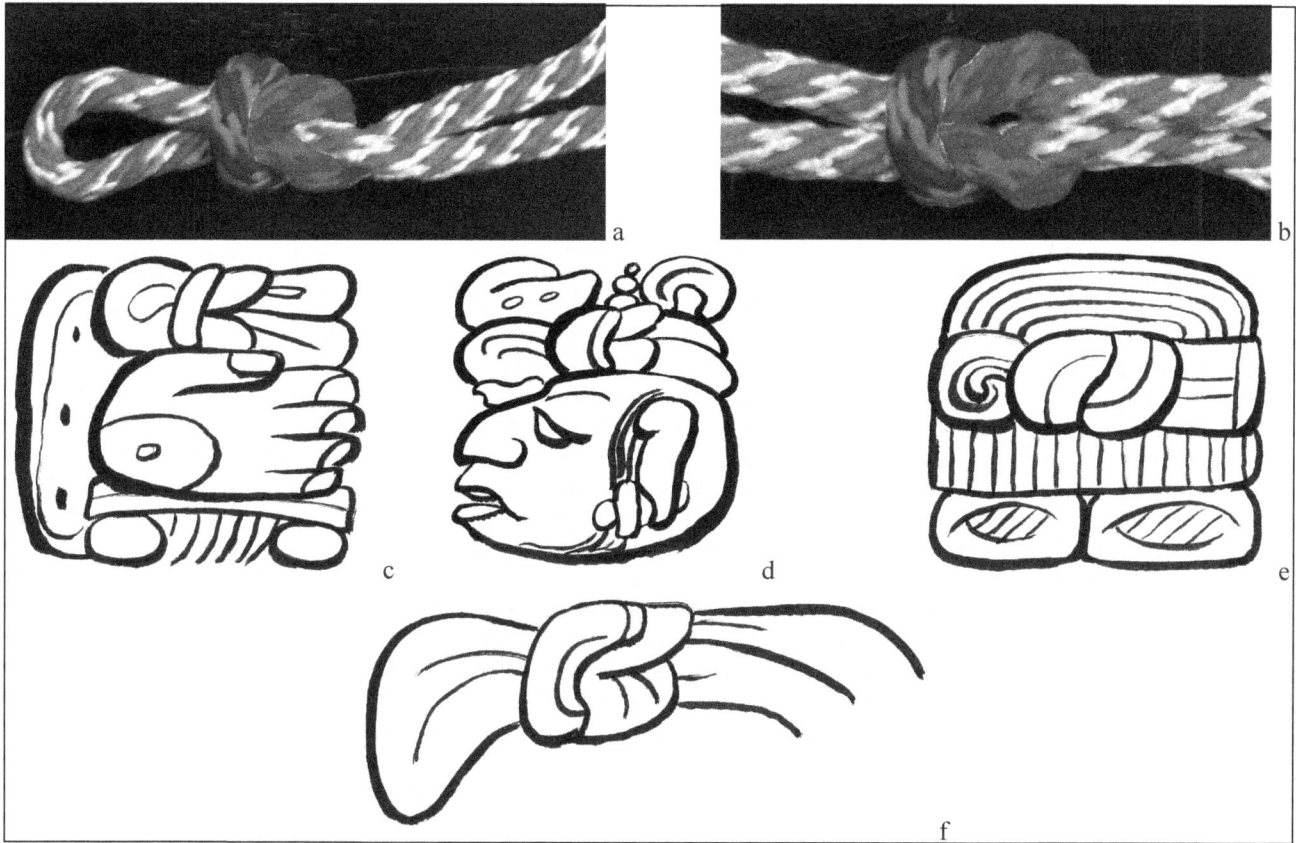

Figure 29: Knots: a) and b) square knots in rope; c) *u k'ahlaj sak huun*; d) *ti' huun*; e) Tikal's Emblem Glyph;
f) knot worn by a historical figure on Palenque Temple XIX altar

Figure 30: *K'al* describing the text wrapping around the rim of a ceramic vessel. (Photograph K1941 © Justin Kerr)

a loop out of the cord that will snare an iguana. Second, *k'al* wraps the headband around the newly inaugurated ruler's head. Third, in the context of hieroglyphic inscriptions on ceramic vessels, *k'al* traces the text along the rim of the cup or plate. (See Figure 30) As we have seen, though, astronomical contexts suggest that there is an abstracted sense of *k'al* in which time 'completes' periods of time. The latter type of 'tracing a closed path' might be best understood by looking at the conceptualization of humanity in Mayan languages.

1.3 ABSTRACTED LOOPS

Mayanists have long suggested that the vigesimal character of the numerical system came from the twenty digits of a person (Aveni 2001:130-132; Coggins 2007:215). Indeed, the Mayan hieroglyphic writing system occasionally employed a single finger as a representation of the number 1.[35] Also, epigraphers have now revised the reading of the elements of the Long Count to include *winik* 'person' as the reading of 20-day periods, and *winikhaab* 'person-year' – '20 year(s)' for what used to be referred to as a k'atun (Stuart 2007:118). A human counting on her/his fingers and toes demonstrates the equivalence of zero and twenty by 'completing,' circling,' or 'enclosing' the person. I follow Thompson in seeing that this equivalence of zero to twenty—this tracing out of a *counted* closed loop—forms the base of the more abstracted calendrical meaning of *k'al* (Thompson 1975:137-139).

The evidence behind this assertion has been reviewed multiple times, albeit not marshaled for this specific argument. David Stuart noticed, for example, that the word for both 'twenty' and 'knot' in Tzeltalan languages is *tab* (1996:155). As we have already seen, the word for twenty in Yucatec is *k'al* (Barrera Vasquez 1995:367)—homophonous to the verb we have been considering throughout this essay. Considering Mayan hieroglyphic representations of 'zero' further evidences the conflation. Very often, scribes used the 'flower'/cosmogram representation within Long Count dates. In other cases, though, (and often at Copan and nearby Quirigua) they used the *k'al* logogram (T713) as a substitute. (See Figure 31) In both cases modern epigraphers would transcribe the number as '0,' but that may be masking the concept, or even reducing it too far (Thompson 1975:138).

Figure 31: *K'al* logogram serving as 'zero' from Quirigua Stela A. (Drawing by Mathew Looper. Permission by M. Looper)

---

[35] See, for example, the Temple XIX throne inscription at Palenque.

There may even be evidence that the concept of "origin = completion"—of tracing a numerical closed loop—even predates the Long Count. The well-known "acrobats" from the Preclassic may form representations of this concept. That is, the acrobat's position is to place his hands on his face and arch his torso backward to place his feet on the back of his head, thus forming a circle. (See Figure 32a) Here, the human extends to form a representation of 20 and so encloses a circular "personified" (qua *winik*) space.[36]

This observation brings us back directly to the verb root *k'al* when we consider a specific acrobat representation, this one a Preclassic sculpture from the Pacific slopes of Guatemala. (See Figure 32b) In this representation, the hands and feet do not meet on the head; here, they are "knotted" together. That is, a single hand replaces the top loop of the square knot, and the feet take the place of the two wrapping elements, giving the connection the same form as the representation of Mayan hieroglyphic paper knots. (Compare Figures 29 & 32b) So as not to suggest a representation that is not contemporaneously attested, we may recognize that the same iconographic form was used for the knots underneath the chin of each of the sculpted figures, holding their "helmets" on, and in profile for the loincloth of the circumferential figure.[37]

I suggest that this figure may be providing an early source behind the idea of *k'al* both in its functional and abstracted senses. At the very least, it sets up a further investigation into the iconography of *k'al*.

1.2 COSMOGRAPHIC LOOPS

K'al as the tracing of a closed loop and its symbolic connection to knots becomes quite productive in reading Mesoamerican cosmology. If the Preclassic monument of Figure 32 gives the human corporeal realization, then we may turn to Alfred Maudslay for entry into the calendric/cosmographic version. In his landmark publication *Biologia Centrali-Americana: Archaeology*, Maudslay drew explicit comparison between the shapes of the Féjérvary-Mayer and Madrid cosmograms and a Mayan hieroglyph. Referring to his Plate XXXII (Figure 33), Maudslay writes:

> "The Maya calendar occurs in the MS. known as the Codex Cortesianus, and the Mexican calendar is taken from plate 44 of the Fejervary Codex… it will be seen that the arrangement of the calendar is in exactly the same shape as the sign which I suppose to be the numeral twenty.

> "If I am right in my suggestion the likeness in the arrangement of the calendar to the numeral twenty

---

[36] See Coggins (2007) for an interesting compilation of connections between the number twenty and humanity's Mesoamerican self-conceptualization.

[37] It may be purely coincidental, but notice that both representations here could be described by Kaufmann's Ixil and Mam terms: *k'alb'il* and *k'alb'al*.

Figure 32a: Preclassic ceramic 'acrobat' figure. (Photograph courtesy of www.mesoamerican-archives.com)

Figure 32b: Preclassic Pacific Coast inscribed stone showing two acrobat figures bearing and taking the shape of knots. (Photography by Jorge Perez de Lara, used by permission)

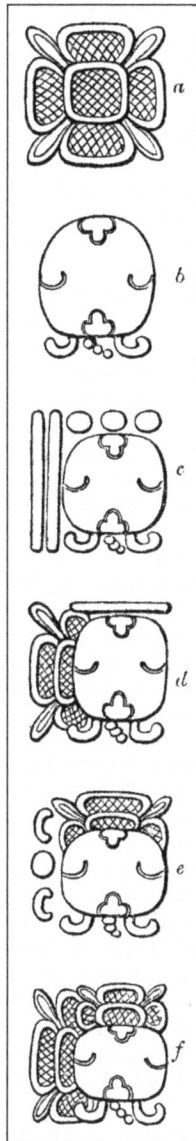

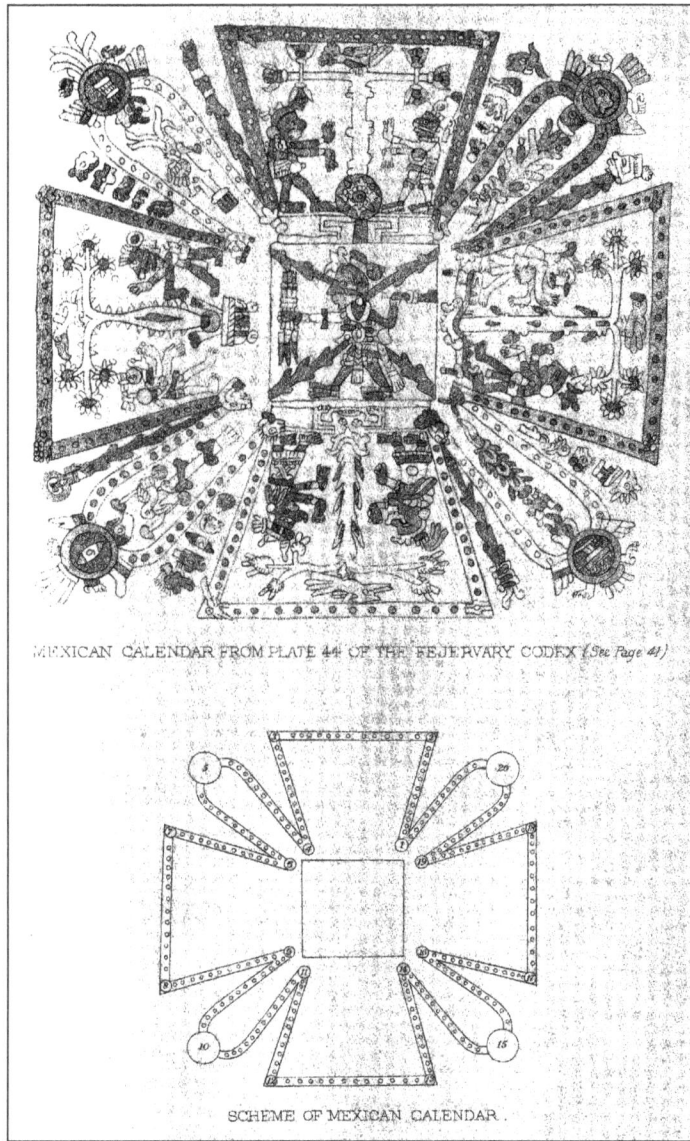

Figure 33: Illustrations from Maudslay's Plate XXXII showing the connection he made between the Mayan glyph for zero/completion and the frontispiece of the Codex Fejervary-Mayer (From the facsimile edition of *Biologia Centrali-Americana* by Alfred P. Maudslay. Published 1974 by Milpatron Publishing Corp., Stamford, CT.)

would suggest a numeration in scores, which is in accordance with what is stated by the early Spanish writers" (1890:41-42).

Here Maudslay is implicitly raising the ambiguity of the number 20 in Mayan hieroglyphic writing, and by extension in Mesoamerican thought. Herbert Spinden and later Eric Thompson both argued that Maudslay's '20' glyph held a value of 'zero' or 'completion,' computationally fitting within Long Count mathematics (Grube and Nahm 1990:15-16). I suggest that the ambiguity between '20' and '0' here is not strictly an error in the logic of either side of this argument; rather, 20, 0, and 'completion' all make sense with reference to the origin of Mayan numeration in the human body as we have seen above. Moreover, a closer look at the Féjérvary-Mayer and Madrid 'cosmograms' and their compositions sheds new light on the concept of *k'al*. (See Figures 34 & 35)

The iconography of the Féjérvary-Mayer image speaks to a sensibility of weaving space and time that is deep and wide in ancient Mesoamerican cultural representation. In the Book of Chilam Balam of Chumayel, we read that:

"after the destruction of the world was completed, they placed <a tree> to set up in its order the yellow cock oriole. Then the white tree of abundance was set up. A pillar of the sky was set up, a sign of the destruction of the world; that was the white tree of abundance in the north. Then the black tree of abun-

dance was set up <in the west> for the black-breasted pix?oy to sit upon. Then the yellow tree of abundance was set up <in the south>, as a symbol of the destruction of the world, for the yellow-breasted pixoy to sit upon, for the yellow cock oriole to sit upon, the yellow timid *mut*. Then the green tree of abundance was set up in the center <of the world> as a record of the destruction of the world" (Roys 1967:100).

Similar "world trees" have been identified at the opposite end of the Mayan temporal spectrum in the murals of San Bartolo (Saturno *et al.* 2004). Even the Borgia Codex on the pages leading up to Seler's Venus pages depict the setting up of cosmic trees accompanied by the passage of the 260-day count (Diaz and Rogers 1993: Plates 48 – 53). One representation of time and cosmic regions in particular, though, brings us back to the desideratum of a new translation for *k'al*.

Page one of the Codex Féjérvary-Mayer contains a picture at the center that bears strong resemblance to the warrior figure on page 49 of the Venus pages. While provocative in many respects (compare Figures 2c and 34) of more import is the overall structure of what Aveni calls the "cosmogram" (2001:150-152). Here again, we see four trees associated with specific birds, each anchored to one side of a central square. The colors red, yellow, black, and blue associate the trapezoidal frames surrounding each tree and the two figures attending it with a specific cosmic region. A step back reveals that the

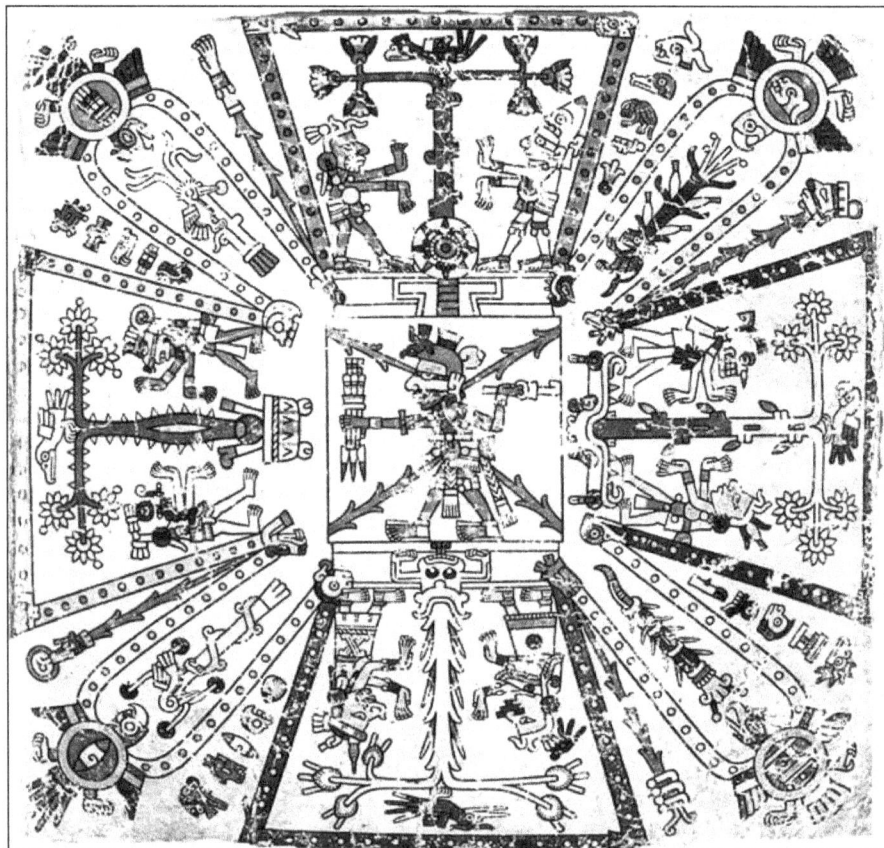

Figure 34: Frontispiece for the Codex Féjérvary Mayer.
(Image is in the public domain; obtained from Wikimedia Commons)

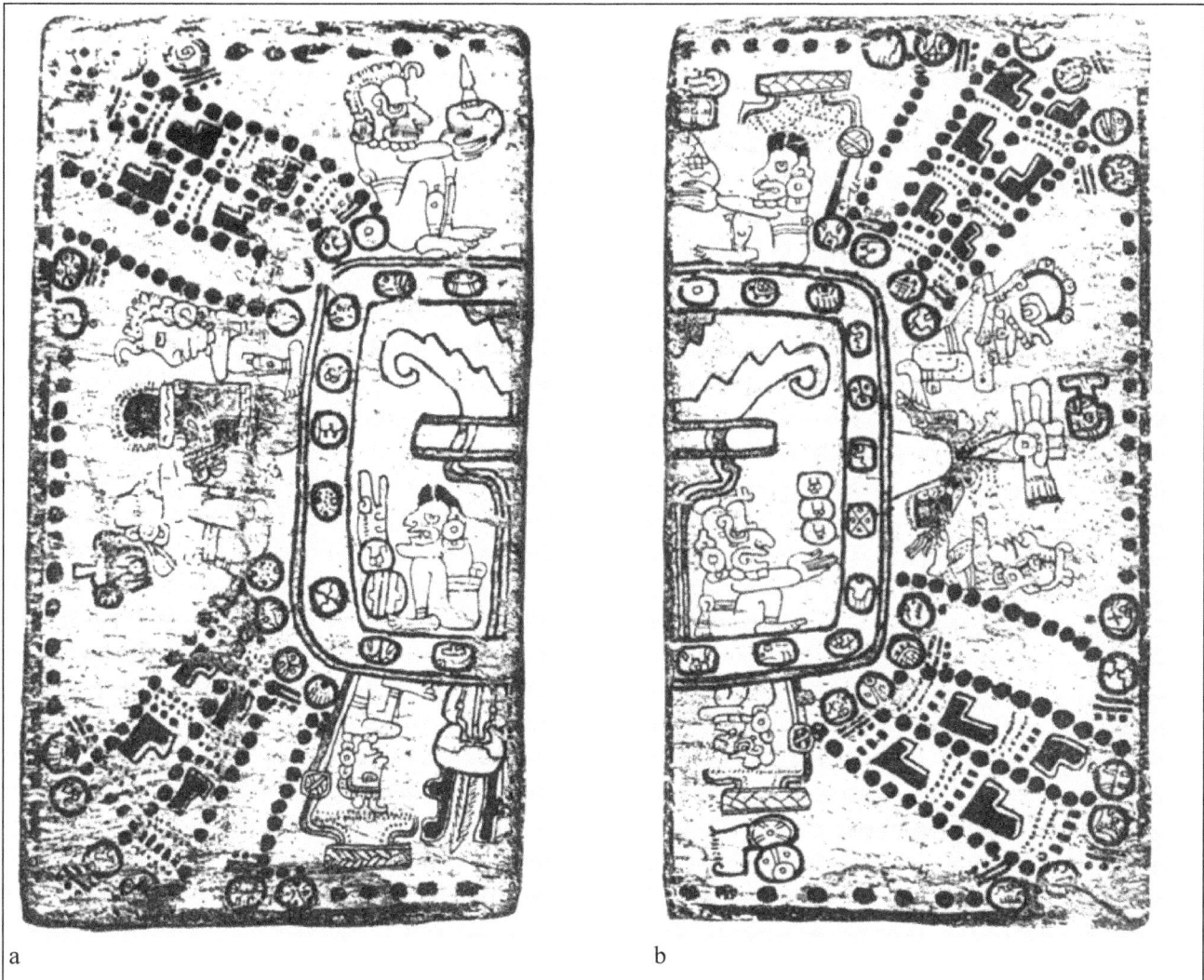

Figure 35: Cosmogram on Pages 75-76 of the Madrid Codex
(courtesy Foundation for the Advancement of Mesoamerican Studies, Inc., www.famsi.org)

trapezoidal regions form a cross pattée[38] augmented with intercardinal lobes, all of which creates a continuous path around the ritual activity. Furthermore, the path that loops around the entire scene is marked by 12 dots on each segment, and each vertex carries a Day Sign from the 260-day count. As with a count of 20 with the human body, Paxton notes that for the Madrid Codex, the path ends with the implication that it could/should start over again (2001:33). That is, the last Day Sign, in the upper right intercardinal lobe, is Tochtli; 12 dots later we return to the first Day Sign, at the base of the upper arm of the cross, Cipactli, where the count began. The straight-forward inference is that in this representation, any dot (representing a date within the 260-day Count) is its own beginning and end in this cycle. The cosmogram is a ritual 'completion' qua 'making whole' of space and time.

This 'tracing of a closed loop' appears to be deeply embedded within Mesoamerican ideology. Meredith Paxton also notes that "Aveni (1980:155-156), León-Portilla (1988:65-66), and Villa Rojas (1988:127-134) have observed that the shape of the tzolkin motif in the Codex Madrid page 75-76 painting is very similar to the Maltese-cross-like diagrams of the world directions made by the modern Maya of Yucatán and other areas" (2001:31). But Paxton also makes reference to William Hanks's work on Yucatecan documents that, coincidentally, considers Mikhail Bakhtin's "kinds of completeness" (1987:672). Hanks takes up a number of official documents written in Yucatec Mayan during the sixteenth century to consider the practices of discourse within them. His focus on Yaxkukul Document 1 is ideal for our purposes here.

Within this document, Hanks recognizes a prose device that he calls "cyclic description" (1987:674). He finds that thirty well-defined cycles completely exhaust lines 111 through 284 of the text. One such cycle he gives from lines 154 – 162:

---

[38] This form is commonly referred to as a Maltese cross in the literature (citations), but for those who study such things, this is an incorrect classification. Rather than having flat ends, the cross members of a Maltese cross have 'v's taken out of them, producing a cross with eight very distinct points (and each point bearing symbolic meaning). The cross pattée is a more general form in which the cross members are wider at their ends than at their centers (citations).

154 nohol-tan yn-bin-el tzol pic-tun
Adv-Adv Apro-Vi-sf Vi N
Southward I go counting out (ordering) boundary
   stones.
155 t-u-lac-al u-bin-el
Prep-Apro-N-sf Apro-Vi-sf
All (the way) it goes
156 la-tu-lah kuch'-ul t-u-chun mul ac
part-?-part Vi-sf Prep-Apro-N N N
until arriving at the foot of Turtle Mount,
157-8 y-an u- / pic-tun-il
Apro-Vs Apro- N-N-sf
(where) there is the boundary stone.
158-9 ti c-in-patt-ic ah cumkal-i
Dloc Aux-Apro-Vt-inc Agt N-trm
There I leave off (the) Cumkal people,
160 ti-ix c-in-ch'a-ic in-yum yxkil ytzam pech
Dloc-conj Aux-Apro-Vi-inc Apro-N Name
there too I pick up (am joined by) my father Ixkil
   Itzam Pech,
161 ah Sic pach' y u-kuch-te-el-ob
Agt Place Name conj Apro-V-N-sf-pl
(who is) from Sicipach and (along with) his counsellors.
162 ca-cath-il / yn-bin-el y-et-el-ob
Rdpl-Num-sf Apro-Vi-sf Apro-RN-sf-pl
Pairwise I proceed accompanied by them ##
(Hanks 1987:674).

Hanks notes that while there is some variation to the
specific order of elements within any specific cycle, the

internal composition of cycles may be said to consist
roughly of the following information: (1)
(inter)cardinal direction of motion in which the
narrator ("I") is said to be proceeding while counting
boundary markers (line 154, 163); (2) name of the
next goal or landmark toward which he is proceeding
(line 156, 164); (3) title or name of nobles who
accompanied the narrator during this segment of his
inspection, along with names of their town of
residence (line 160-161); (4) the location of the
boundary markers relative to landmark wells, trees,
roads, or "corners" (line 157, 166); (5) the place at
which accompanying nobles leave off and new ones
join him (lines 159-162). (1987:674-675)

Overall, then, the narrative charts out a large square
oriented to the cosmic regions. As the narrator proceeds
along the sides of the square, one or more representatives
of that region accompany him. Changing direction, his
accompaniment changes as well. The parallel to the
Madrid and Féjérvary-Mayer Codices, therefore, is clear,
with the exception that the narrator is processing along a
geographic path, not a temporal (i.e. 260-day Count) one.

But Hanks's purpose is other than a consideration of
continuity with Precontact scribal traditions (which he
does not mention explicitly at all). Instead, Hanks reveals
an underlying structure that is just as useful. That is, he
suggests that there is an ordering structure behind this
type of textual record—a Bourdieuean habitus—that is
instantiated through the need for a legitimate document

(1987:670-671). In this case, part of the document's
legitimacy comes from its invocation of the cyclic
description prose device.

Beyond its linguistic utility, though, such cyclicity works
perfectly with the interpretation of a cosmogram as *k'al*
described above. That is, as a ritual habitus, a narrative
expression of cyclicity would come directly from an
ideology anchored to *k'al*. *K'al* is not just a physical
tracing out of a closed path—it may have been
ideological as well. Making the case even stronger,
Hanks identifies what he considers to be the same
practice in a separate manuscript also of the sixteenth
century. Here, he refers to a Sotuta land survey document
and its use of graphic elements as substitutes for or
complements to words:

The discourse has a strong iconic component, not in
cyclicity like the Yaxkukul documents, but in the use,
within the written text, of a graphic representation of
the crosses. Thirteen maltese crosses appear in the
list, as illustrated in excerpt 2.

2. Excerpt from Sotuta land documents (Roys
   1939:425-426):
   tisidzbi, tiiximche +, Tzuck,[...] cansahcab donde
      estaba una + cruz,[…]
   Tisidzbic, Tiiximche CROSS, Tzuck, .. Cansahcab
      where there was a CROSS cross.
   Tixkochah donde estaba una +
   Tixkochah where there was a CROSS

The three tokens of the cross displayed in excerpt 2
show three different syntactic incorporations of the
symbol into the written text. In the first case, it
appears without accompanying verbal description,
implying that a cross was placed at the Tiiximche, but
not stating this in words. The second instance of the
symbol occurs within the noun phrase "a cross,"
illustrating what is also stated in the verbal discourse.
In the third example, the graphic symbol substitutes
for a lexical noun in the noun phrase "a _ ." Hence, a
graphic representation may entirely replace
description or may be integrated into it as a
reinforcement or partial substitute (1987:675).

It does not hurt the argument here that the first cross is
located at Tiiximche, which translates to 'at the maize
tree' since, for example, the Borgia has the central tree as
a maize plant.[39] More importantly, though, when we
recognize that this narrative is tracing out a closed path,
we realize that the crosses function as synecdoche. That
is, both the narrative and the geographic path enclose
ritual space and so are symbolized by the textual and
physical crosses.

This is not an isolated case. Another colonial Yucatecan
document also made suggestive use of the cross pattée
within a geographic description. The paragraph quoted

---

[39] The Book of Chilam Balam also notes that the central tree is the
"green tree of abundance," which might easily be construed as a maize
plant (Roys 19XX:YY).

above recounting the setting up of the world trees in the Book of Chilam Balam of Chumayel ended with a cross pattée icon (1967:100). The delimitation of the cosmos, therefore, was punctuated with this *k'al* symbol, further binding the account to the conceptualization found in the Féjérvary-Mayer and Madrid cosmograms to the Mayan hieroglyphic representation (T173). Within the Roys translation, there are only four of these cross pattée icons noted in the Chumayel manuscript. The world tree passage contains one of them; the other three are all built into the k'atun wheel prophecies (1967:132, 146, 155). The k'atun wheel also is oriented according to the cosmic regions.

When it comes to the tracing of a closed path in ritual time and space, that path takes the form of the *pattée* cross.

This colonial material explicitly raises the issue of geographic processions associated with the cross pattée cosmogram and so with *k'al*. In fact, we have already seen this from the Classic period. The wall texts in Copan Structure 10L-11 set up a path for the coherent reading of the distributed narrative. This path itself formed a cross pattée. (See Figure 16) Each reading constituted a ritual tracing of the cosmic regions from the temple, and each completed reading implied the beginning of another. Symbolically, then, these texts were ritually enclosing the cosmos—but, again, this should not be surprising given the cosmic themes long identified within its decoration (Fash 1991:168; Miller 1988; Schele and Freidel 1990: 323-328; Newsome 2001:50-51)

1.1 *K'ALTUUN*: THE OUTLIER

Now, it would be tempting and relatively straightforward at this point to further suggest that the practices in the Yaxkukul and Sotuta documents were simply descendent versions of Classic period *k'altuun* ceremonies, i.e. that stones were set up along the boundaries of towns and processions from one to the next constituted 'stone-enclosings.' We might even like to see the great carved stelae as these markers. For one, though, Hanks explicitly negates the possibility: "[a]ccording to Gaspar Antonio Chi... the preconquest Maya observed no boundaries within provinces, but did maintain boundaries between provinces" (Chi, in Tozzer 1941:230; Hanks 1987:689). No boundaries between towns in the same province means no need for boundary markers around a given town.

Besides Chi's authoritative statement, archaeologically, no such regularly placed stones have been recovered from Classic period sites. So, if *k'altuuns* were not the stones used to define a cosmic boundary, are we forced to accept that the *k'al* in *k'altuun* is somehow not part of the ritual coherence we developed above?

Actually, it is here that David Stuart's 1996 speculations come to our aid. In his consideration of the *k'altuun* ceremony—the one generating the stone-binding

interpretation—Stuart hinted at an idea that brings this all together. His initial thoughts in assessing the absence of stelae at specific sites along the Usumacinta referred to small stones that may have been used to count time.

> Curiously, the sites of Palenque and Pomona, which feature the numbered *tun* counts... were not in the custom of erecting stelae or large outdoor altars. Clearly some other type of 'stone' must be alluded to, perhaps even smaller types of ritual stones such as jade beads or pebbles (reminiscent of the small stones [that] are used by modern day-keepers and diviners) although this would be impossible to verify (Stuart 1996:151).

I suggest that "impossible" is too strong a word here. In fact, there is evidence he could have used to support this thesis. This evidence becomes recognizable in the numerous "pecked crosses" found throughout ancient Mesoamerica (Aveni 2001:329-334). (See Figure 36) Aveni summarizes, in his extensive studies of them, that they frequently possess a total of 260 dots, and often contain sub-sections that sum to 20 and 18—important factors of the *haab* (2001:331). He notes further that "[t]he axes of several cross petroglyphs correlate very well with solstice positions, and a solar symbolism is strongly suggested" (2001:332) With axes oriented to the solstices, the circular portions would symbolically enclose the four cosmic regions.

Aveni further describes Teotihuacan no. 2 cross: "[f]ound in the floor of a building along the Street of the Dead, this triple concentric design takes the shape of a Maltese Cross" (2001:331). He then describes the pattern of dots, which amounts to 4 arms, each comprising a sequence of $13 + 1 + 18 + 1 + 18 + 1 + 13 = 65$; $4 \times 65 = 260$.[40] (See Figure 36) I suggest that by moving a small stone from one dimple to the next within this pattern, that stone would trace around both the region and the time period and so *the stone* would have been a *k'altuun*.

Yet we are not restricted to inference here. Stuart also referred to Barrera Vasquez's entry for the term *k'atun*, which he saw as derived from *k'al-tuun* (1996:155-156). Referring to the personal compilations and considerations of William Brito Sansores, Barrera Vasquez records the following under the first definition of **K'ATUN**:

> 13*wbs*: por los renglones anteriores puede uno darse cuenta que no hay un significado claro o firme para la palabra **k'atun**, pues mientras la fuente 1 dice que 'es una especie de veinte años', la fuente 8 informa de un período de 13 años, en lo que sí están de acuerdo todos los estudiosos es que **k'atun** significa 'cierre de período de tiempo' ya que **k'al tun** significa 'piedra-que-cierra'; para mayor claridad pasamos a traducir algunos terminus relativos que nos da la fuente 8: **k'in k'atun**: cierre de período de días; **ahaw k'atun:**

---

[40] Aveni records the pattern as: "1 + 18 + 1 + 13 + 13 + 1 + 18 + 1 + 18 + 1 + 13 + 13 + ... = 260" (2001:331). Based on the verbal description, though, it is clear that he simply left out the necessary additional "1 + 18" from the beginning of this equation.

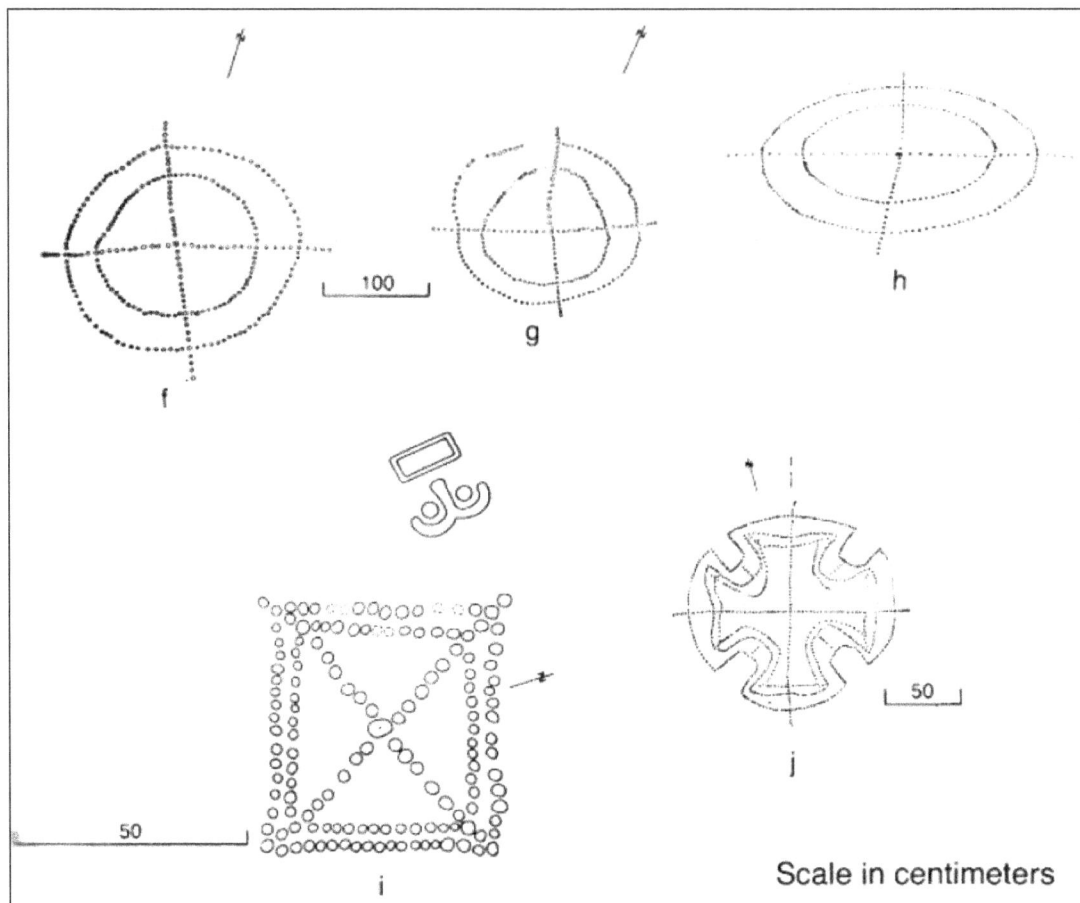

Figure 36: Pecked crosses throughout Mesoamerica examined (image courtesy of Anthony Aveni)

k'atun real; **wak'atun** [**u ah k'atun**]: **k'atun** lunar; en lo que parece haber más claridad es que los números 13 y 20 tienen importante papel en el concepto **k'atun** ya que pueden ser 13 **winales** de a 20 días o veinte trecenas de 20 días; lo que nos induce a pensar que puede llamárse también **k'atun** al año de 260 días, llamado año sagrado, que quizá sea el **u ah k'atun** o **k'atun** lunar a que se refiere Don Juan Pío Pérez (Barrera Vasquez 1995:386).

Brito Sansores glosses *k'altuun* as "piedra-que-cierra"—'stone that closes'—and *k'atun* as 'cierre de período de tiempo'—'close of a period of time.' These together directly corroborate the *k'altuun* as the stone traversing the pecked crosses. Note, though, that there is also a *k'in k'atun* and a *u ah k'atun*—closings of solar and lunar periods. These directly parallel the *k'alk'in* and Glyph C hieroglyphic uses we have seen above. Rather than look for a single referent, then, I suggest that it makes more sense to see a *k'altuun* as a stone that has traced out a closed loop in space and time—a time period of *any* length.

And, in fact, this interpretation resolves another of Stuart's open questions.

Nahuatl *xihuitl* and Maya *tun* seem to be related in their common meanings of both 'precious stone' and 'year.' *Xiuhmohpilli*, [*sic*] equally translatable as the

'binding of precious stones,' referred to the rite of cosmic renewal at the close of the fifty-two year cycle, when the 'new fire' was drilled at midnight atop the hill of Citlaltepec. ... If a connection to the Maya *k'altun* rite exists, it would have to be a distant one, of course, for the Mexica ceremony was centered upon the fifty-two-year cycle of the Calendar Round and not the Maya concept of the twenty-year k'atun; the two cultures were separate in both time and space. However, there is enough ideological continuity in the Mesoamerican culture to render this similarity an interesting one (1996:158).

The above argument that the process of stone-enclosing does not need to be tied to a specific time period resolves Stuart's quandary. Actually, though, we do not need to rely on this argument; a direct response comes from a careful reading of Bernardino de Sahagun's description of the *xiuhmolpilli*.

For at that time (these years) were piled up, added one to another, and brought together; wherefore the thirteen-year (cycles) and four times made a circle, as hath been made known. Hence was it said that then were tied and bound our years, and that once again the years were newly laid hold of. When it was evident that the years lay ready to burst into life, everyone took hold of them, so that once more would start forth—once again—another (period of) fifty-two years. Then (the two cycles) might proceed to reach one hundred and four years. It was called "One Old Age" *when twice they had made the round, when twice the times of binding the years had come together* (1953, p. 25) (Aveni 2001:148; emphasis added).

This essay argues that the specific "cycles" and "counts" could easily have been those determined by the movement of stones around a pecked, painted, or carved calendric trace. The key, though, is that the time period itself was not the referent. Any of these procedures were *k'altuun* activities because in each case, the movement of stones traced out time periods.

Now it is not difficult at this point to see a potential link between small stones enclosing periods and immobile monumental stelae. That is, venturing into more speculative interpretation, we may conceive of a public stela serving as a symbolic representation of the small stone tracing out the temporal loop. As Stuart suggested, this would make sense of the fact that some Classic period cities made extensive use of stelae, while others did not, yet they all recorded numerous *k'altuun* or *chumtuun* events (1996:151). Understood in this way, the erection of a stela to commemorate the enclosing would have been optional even though the event itself would have taken place. This hypothetical link between stelae and small manipulable loop-tracing stones may find support from two distinct lines of evidence.

The first possibility comes from the precursors of Classic Mayan stelae: incised celts. The default form of *k'al* is the hand holding a celt, or a polished object (Schele and Miller). This may suggest that the earliest *k'al* activities involved the moving of a polished jade stone from one position to the next around a calendric path. It may also be that the stones marking the larger periods being counted were not simply pebbles.

The Leiden Plaque is an Early Classic incised celt carrying one of the earliest recorded Long Count dates (8.14.3.1.12 1 Eb 0 Yaxk'in). (See Figure 37) The very short text accompanying the date provides a provocative narrative couplet. The seating of the month is compositionally, conceptually, and representationally paired with the seating of the ruler. Specifically, the text reads **CHUM-mu YAX-K'IN CHUM-la-ja** [ruler's name] – 'Yaxk'in sits. The ruler takes a seated position.' This stone, then, marks the layered beginning of a period—a period of solar time and the period of the ruler's reign. This celt itself, then, could have been an early *k'al tuun*. It may have been 'seated' to mark the beginning of calendric periods proceeding therefrom. Over time, and with more resources at a ruler's disposal, such hand-held celts may have been transformed into monumental stelae carved from volcanic tuff.

Such an interpretation leads to a second possible source of evidence. That is, rulers are often dressed as identifiable deities on Period Ending stelae. This is especially true for Waxaklajun Ub'aah K'awiil, thirteenth ruler of

Copan. If a period counted by a *k'altuun* corresponded to a cosmic period like one of those in the Féjérvary-Mayer and Madrid cosmograms, the ruler may have been impersonating the deity corresponding to the count and the region enclosed. Under this interpretation, the deities he impersonated would have corresponded to the figures in the lobes of a diagram such as the Féjérvary-Mayer or the Madrid Codices. This is venturing into deep speculation, but it might take a hypothetical form through a large-scale study comparing the deity representations of rulers on Period Ending marking stelae.

On the other hand, the texts on these monuments are very provocative. The well-known Stela A, for example, carries a passage that has been puzzling for some time. Moving from an obscure event enacted by Waxaklajun Ub'aah K'awiil, thirteenth ruler of Copan, on the back of Stela A, the narrative notes the future 4 Ajaw 13 Yax, 15th katun end. This leads to the bottom row of glyphs, which are eroded, but seem to refer to a makom tree **ma-ko-?** before picking up again on the south side (See Figure 38):

... xa-MAN-na ma-ko-ma HA'-o-b'a 4-te-CHAN-na 4-?-CHAN-na 4-ni-CHAN-na 4-NAL(?)-CHAN-na [Copan] K'UHUL-AJAW MUTUL-K'UHUL-AJAW-wa ka-KAN-K'UHUL-AJAW-wa B'AAKAL-K'UHUL-AJAW-wa AJAW/pa-ni-yi-li [celt]-CHAN-na [celt]-K'AB-la EL-K'IN-ni OCH'-K'IN-ni ma-?-?-? xa-MAN-na HA'-o-b'a pa-sa no-ma CH'EN(?)-ya b'a-ka no-ma CH'EN-ya ti-TANLAM [eroded]

'...north makom tree. These four [type-1] skies, four [type-2] skies, four [type-3] skies, four [type-4] skies.... Copan K'uhulajaw, Mutul K'uhulajaw, Kan K'uhulajaw, B'aakal K'uhulajaw. [celt]-Sky. [celt]-Earth. East, West, South, North. [Because of] these, the cave will open, the cave will close on the half-period end.'[41]

A northern tree, four distinct groups of four skies, and four rulers with further reference to the four cosmological regions and a ritual cave—all of this could come together nicely under a reading of four astronomically driven 'loop tracings' supervised by the four most prominent rulers of the day.[42]

Irregardless of these final hypotheses regarding the specific relationships between stelae and manipulable counting stones, we now have a proposal for a single reading of the various instances of *k'al*—we do not have to change its definition based on its context. Just as the *k'al sak huun* used a paper headband to trace a loop around one's head, *k'alb'al* traces a loop around one's waist, and *k'al a chulul* sets a snare for an iguana, the *k'altuun* would have used a stone to trace a loop constituted by a period of time.

---

[41] See Stuart (2006 [notebook]:63) and Lacadena (2004:174) for contributions to this reading, especially with respect to the passive forms.

[42] See also Aldana (2006) for an historical hypothesis that correlates well with this reading.

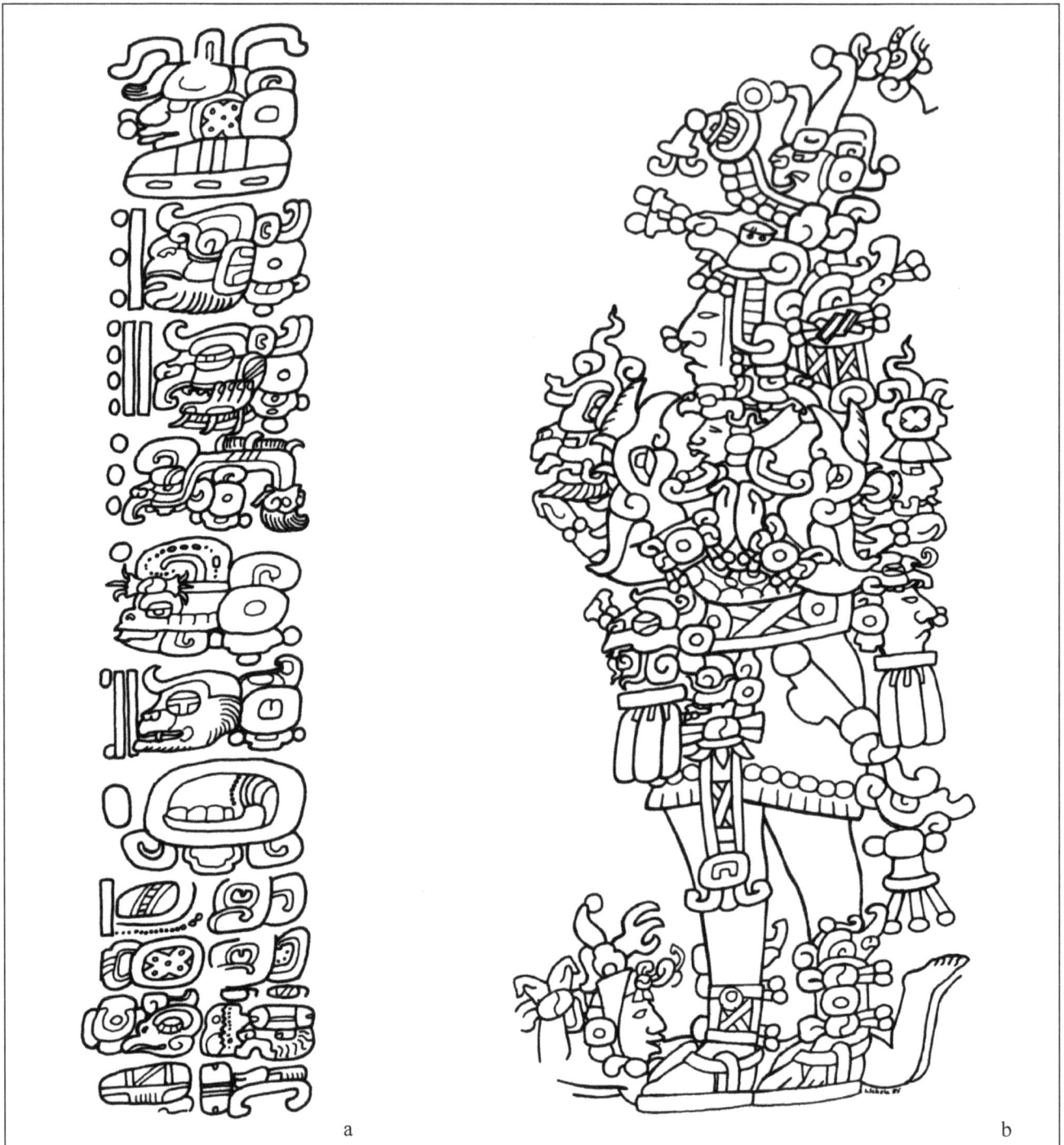

Figure 37: The Leiden Plaque showing the **CHUM** 'seating' metaphor for both the month and the ruler's inauguration. (Drawing by Linda Schele, © David Schele, courtesy Foundation for the Advancement of Mesoamerican Studies, Inc., www.famsi.org)

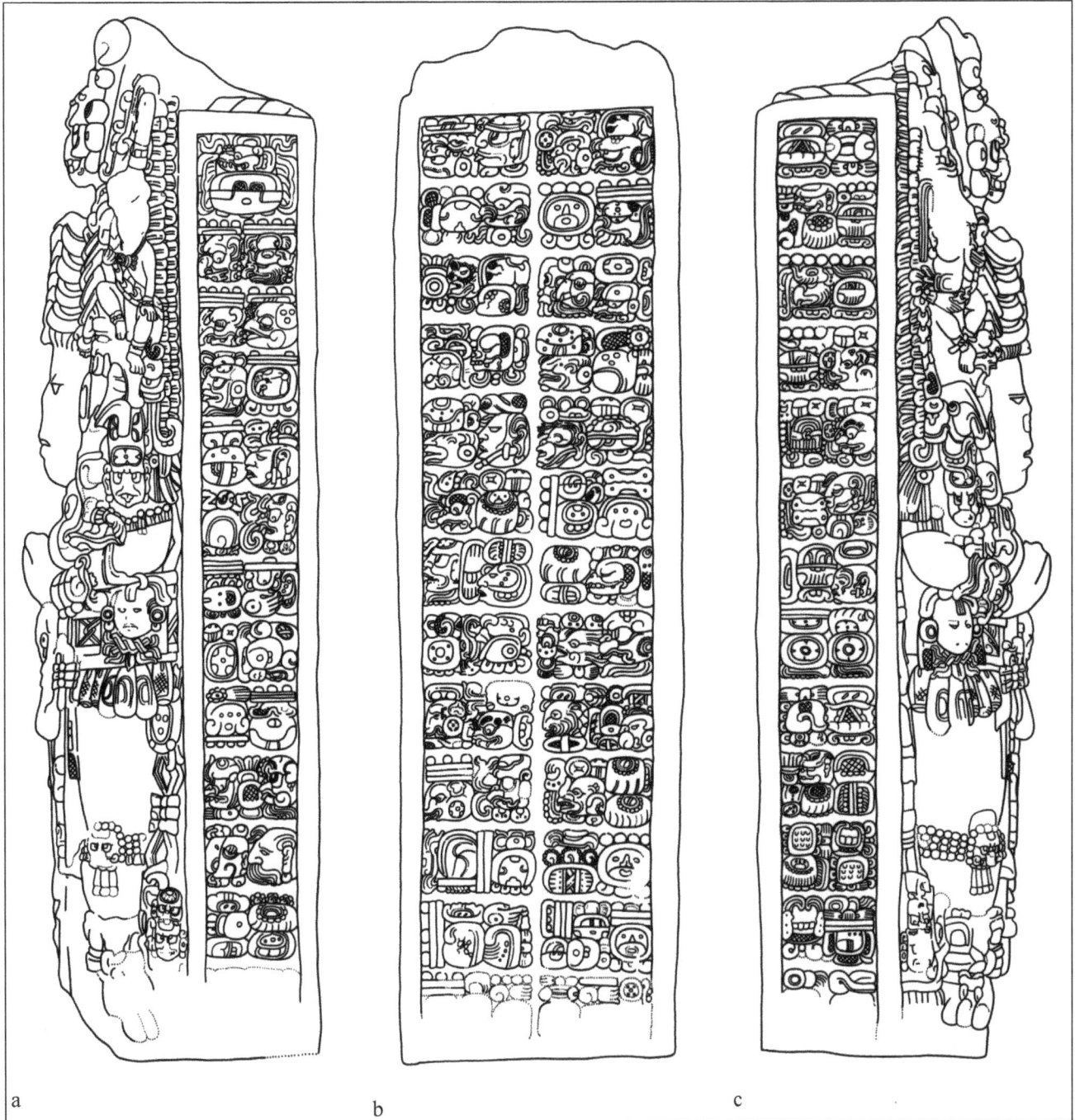

Figure 38: hieroglyphic inscription of Copan Stela A. The text on the right describes four types of four skies and relates them to the ajawtahk of Copan, Tikal, Calakmul, and Palenque as well as the four cosmic regions, East, West, South, and North. (Drawing by Linda Schele, © David Schele, courtesy Foundation for the Advancement of Mesoamerican Studies, Inc., www.famsi.org)

CONCLUSION/COMPLETION, THE DOLL AT THE CENTER

At its core, this study has undertaken a reassessment of the verb root *k'al* in both its royal ritual and calendric ceremonial contexts. We have found that a single translation makes sense of all of the contexts in which it has thus far been found, from ceramic vessel texts to white headband accessions, from lunar period records to Long Count coefficients. Therefore, along with the above revised interpretation of the calendrics within the Dresden Codex Venus Table, we are now in a position to reconstruct the role of the textual passages within the Venus pages and so answer the question that initiated this essay. In the end, then, we find that this study has been less like a stack of Russian dolls, and more like the tracing of a closed path that it purports to reveal.

Here, we may turn to Meredith Paxton's work on the *Yucatec Cosmos* to get us started. With the aim of identifying the role of the tropical year in the Dresden Codex Venus Table, Paxton suggested a connection between it and the cosmogram of the Madrid Codex.

> When the pattern of the Madrid illustration is superimposed on the Dresden Venus table, three of its celestial regents can be related to the principal deities and directions in the ideal map of the cosmos. The reading of the Venus table associated with 11.0.3.11.0 1 Ahau 13 Mac base presents two of the regents as incarnations of the winter and summer solstice Suns. The solstices are symbolized in the Madrid 76-75 diagram as the footprints of the Sun. Midway between the solstice markers at the corners of the eastern side of the universe, the Madrid painting represents the Sun God and the young Moon Goddess in the equinox position. In the Dresden table, the regency of the young Moon Goddess connects visibility of Venus as morning star with the vernal equinox; her position in that directional diagram is also in the center of the eastern side (Paxton 2001:95).

We can now look beyond Paxton's solar impetus to realize that the structure of the Madrid Codex cosmogram does not need to be superimposed on the Dresden Codex

Venus Table; it is already in it. Through a reading of *k'al* as 'looping' or 'tracing a closed loop,' we find that the Venus Table of the Dresden Codex does in hieroglyphic text what the Madrid and the Féjérvary-Mayer do with illustrations.

First off, it is straightforward to recognize that the cosmic orientation is the same across codices. The sequence of cross pattée loops is the same in both cases: the count around the Féjérvary-Mayer and the Madrid Codices begins with the East and then moves counter-clockwise around the North, West, and South; likewise, the Venus Table is anchored to the East and then records the *k'al* events of the North, West, and South before returning to the East. (See Figures 2 & 3)

Second, it is the sub-periods of the larger complete round that are marked with Day Signs. In the cosmograms, the Day Signs are positioned so as to sit at the vertices of each 'loop,' and each loop is performed around a cosmological region. (See Figures 34 & 35) These two characteristics are precisely what are described in the Venus Table if we consider a revised reading of the *k'ahlaj* passages. That is, in comparison to the Féjérvary-Mayer and the Madrid images, we may reconsider the grammatical analysis of the repetitive *k'ahlaj* phrase and see that *lak'in* may not be in a sentential position; it very well may be the absolutive of the passive verb *k'ahlaj*. That is, the grammar allows us to see the East as the entity that 'is looped' (**K'AL-ja la-K'IN-ni X CHAK EK'** → *k'a[h]l-aj-Ø lak'in. X, Chak Ek'* → loop-[PASS]-3SA East. X, Venus). Here, the cosmic region is the subject of the passive verb and the 260-day count is provoking the activity.

Notice, though, that this move specifically frees up the role of Venus. In the Féjérvary-Mayer and the Madrid 260-day count cosmological loops, multiple agents are involved. These figures must be important to the ritual enclosing of time and space, but they are not the specific tracers or tracees. Accordingly, Venus and the various other deities are not explicitly acted upon by *k'al*.

Certainly Venus is critical here, but the agent of the activity is time as the 260-Day Count. Such a reading further resolves the otherwise incoherence demonstrated in Table 3. This allows us to see that X and Chak Ek' are involved—and in fact they appear to get enclosed as well, as noted in the Copan text—but they are not identified as the same entity.

Furthermore, under this reading of *k'al*, it is completely reasonable for there to be two *k'al* statements for the same region; *k'al* as 'loop tracing' does not require that Venus be identified on Page 48 with either the Moon Goddess or Tawiskal.[43] Tawiskal as the God of Frost may be authorized by Venus to conduct his spearing without having to become (an aspect of) Venus.

Now there is a difference here between the Féjérvary-Mayer representation and the Dresden in that each of the lobes of the cross in the former contains a different set of deities, whereas in the latter, Chak Ek' shows up in all *k'al* events. On the other hand, this pattern for Chak Ek' does parallel the ritual in the Yaxkukul document described by Hanks. There, the same actor moves through all cosmic regions, but his companions change at each inter-cardinal point. Such would be the role of Venus in the Dresden Codex.

Assuming that this essay's argument is coherent to this point, we may very well be left with one final question: if the Venus pages were intended to describe in hieroglyphic text the imagery of the Féjérvary-Mayer and the Madrid, why did the authors of the Dresden Codex not simply illustrate the images? Why did these Postclassic Mayan scribes not draw out the loop-tracings with the various figures rather than put the whole thing in tabular form?

The answer, I suggest, is rather subtle. The problem is not simply that each region is loop-traced by a different number of days—this could have been handled, for example, by an unequal spacing of dots along the trace. The problem is that a two-dimensional image cannot depict the entire set of loops without introducing visual breaks in the trace. That is, because a single Venus Round encloses all four cosmic regions, yet 584 is not an integer multiple of 260, the Day Signs change five times over a 2,920-day period. Figure 39 shows how the trace could have been maintained continuous in a three-dimensional representation, but that is hardly a realistic suggestion for ancient Mayan scribal art forms.

On the other hand, Figure 40 shows how an image could have captured the enclosings if: i) a visual break in the trace were acceptable; and ii) square images were a

Figure 39: Hypothetical 3-D version of a calendric looping that would accommodate the Venus Cycle

legitimate formatting option. Notice, though, that even here, if the scribes wanted to faithfully represent all of the text on the Venus pages, a significant amount of information would have to be added to each image. Specifically, the omens described in the texts of the right-hand sides of Pages 46 – 50 would have to find further accommodation. So too would we need a means of representing the lower section of text on the left-hand side—the text that we have seen probably described the revision of the table in the distant future. The answer to the text-versus-image question, I propose, is that the tabular format makes for a much more efficient use of space within the codex.[44] The author may well have entertained the possibility, but in the end chose a format more in line with the content of the codex.

The Venus pages of the Dresden Codex have a long history of concerted investigation. By the 1930s, though, Förstemann, Seler, and Teeple proposed most of what has become the standard interpretation of these pages. We might have expected, therefore, that a reconsideration of these pages through the insights produced by the

---

[43] This may also be the reference for one of the few other explicit statements of a *k'ahwan* event. At Palenque, Kan B'ahlam dedicated the Cross Group as his primary construction project, and included an inscription referring to a sequence of *k'al* events. Kan B'ahlam records a *k'ahwan* event enacted by himself and the Sun, witnessed by (or in the presence of) GI. In the image at the center of the tablet bearing this inscription, Kan B'ahlam is shown in a similar position to that taken by the figures on the front page of the Codex Féjérvary-Mayer, who are enclosed within the 260-Day Count.

[44] This recognition of additional information accompanying the enclosings of the Féjérvary-Mayer and Madrid Codices raises for me the possibility of seeing Seler's Venus pages in the Borgia Codex within a new light. Specifically, pages 48 – 53 of the Borgia Codex show world trees like those of the Féjérvary-Mayer cosmogram representing each cosmic region. Above these tree scenes are images of celestial figures, and Day Signs run throughout the imagery. Now, the Day Signs that frame each of the Venus-warrior scenes on Pages 53 and 54 are all at the bottom of Page 48—the page corresponding to the East. If each of these warrior images corresponds to first morning appearance (as all astronomical interpretations agree upon), then the spearings are associated with the East. The other Day Signs for each image are similarly associated with different cosmic regions, but neither the intervals between them nor the patterns amongst them match those of the Dresden Codex. On the other hand, this section of the Borgia Codex ends with an image of the Wind Teotl backed up against a Death Teotl, both enclosed by the 260-Day Count. I suggest that there is much to be explored here that may further tie this section of the Borgia Codex to Pages 46 through 50 of the Dresden Codex.

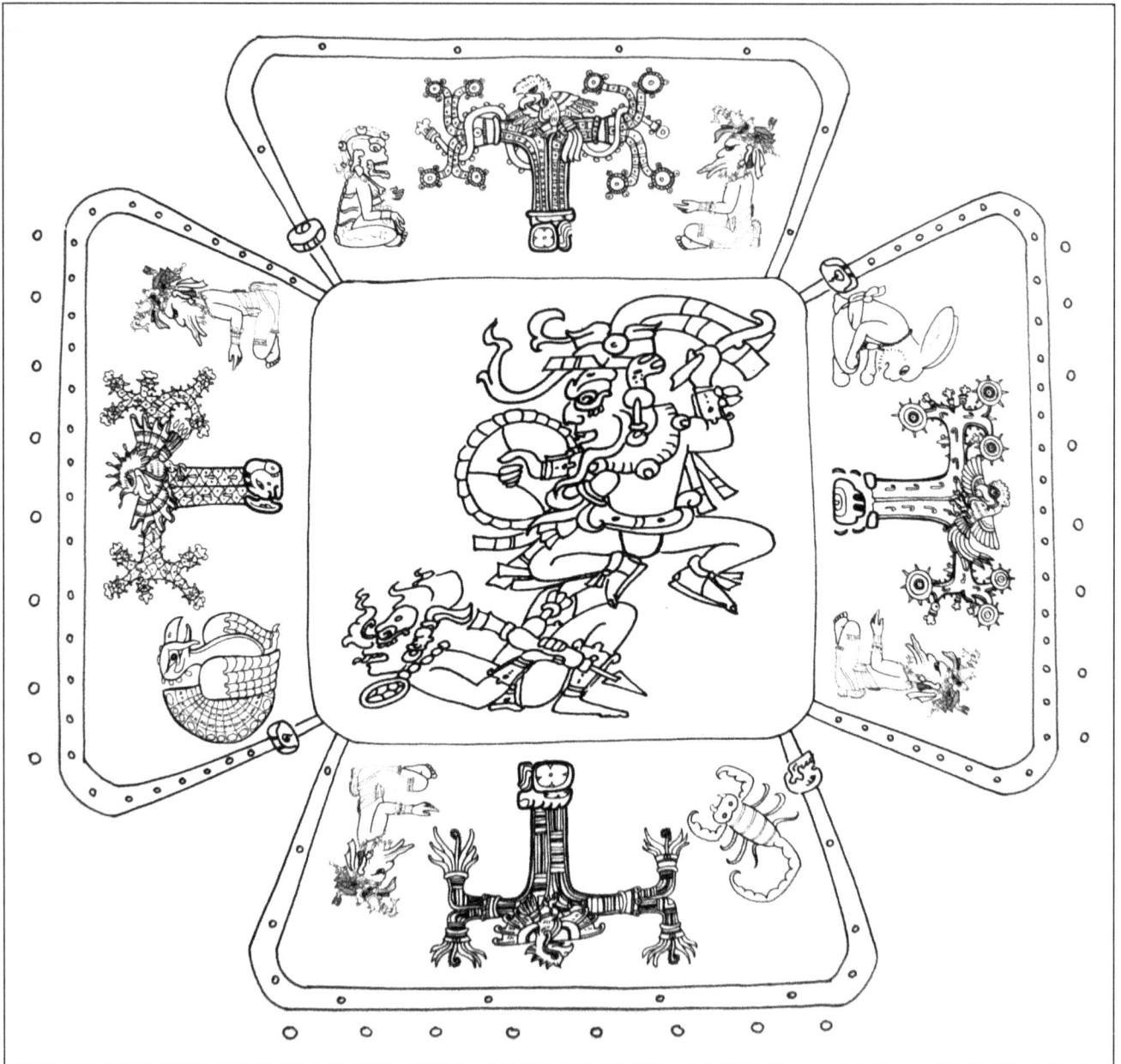

Figure 40a: Graphic representation of the Dresden Codex Venus Table, Pages 46,
according to the interpretation of K'AL presented in this manuscript

hieroglyphic decipherment would suggest a substantial revision. This paper has taken advantage of the breadth of prior study, yet exploited the incongruities left by modern scholarship to propose a new interpretation represented in Figure 40.

Specifically, this paper began with a rather subtle difference in interpreting the verb *k'al* in the Dresden Codex Venus Table versus its appearance in other contexts. Unpacking that subtlety led to a demonstration that either interpretation resulted in conflicting statements about the identity of Venus. An interest in resolving this incoherence through external appeal set up an alternative to previous interpretations of the linguistics, calendrics, and concepts within the Dresden Codex Venus Table. The result places the Mayan calendric treatment of Venus in line with treatments of the Sun and Moon, and it demonstrates a coherence to codical representations across word and image. Indeed, this new reading has even hinted at a time-conditioned habitus revealed in the documents of colonial Yucatan, suggesting practices of discourse spanning Precontact through Colonial times. Furthermore, while it strongly suggests we question the convenience of the day-for-day correlation of the GMT, it rewards us with new insight into ritual time-space within Mesoamerican elite cultures. Indeed, the accumulated data reviewed here, along with that assembled by Seler and others suggests that when we are considering 'time,' we must not limit ourselves to only seeing greatest continuity between the Classic and Postclassic Mayan periods; we must also acknowledge—as scholars have argued cyclically over the last century on iconographic levels—the continuity across geographic and cultural distances as well.

Figure 40b: Graphic representation of the Dresden Codex Venus Table, Pages 47,
according to the interpretation of K'AL presented in this manuscript

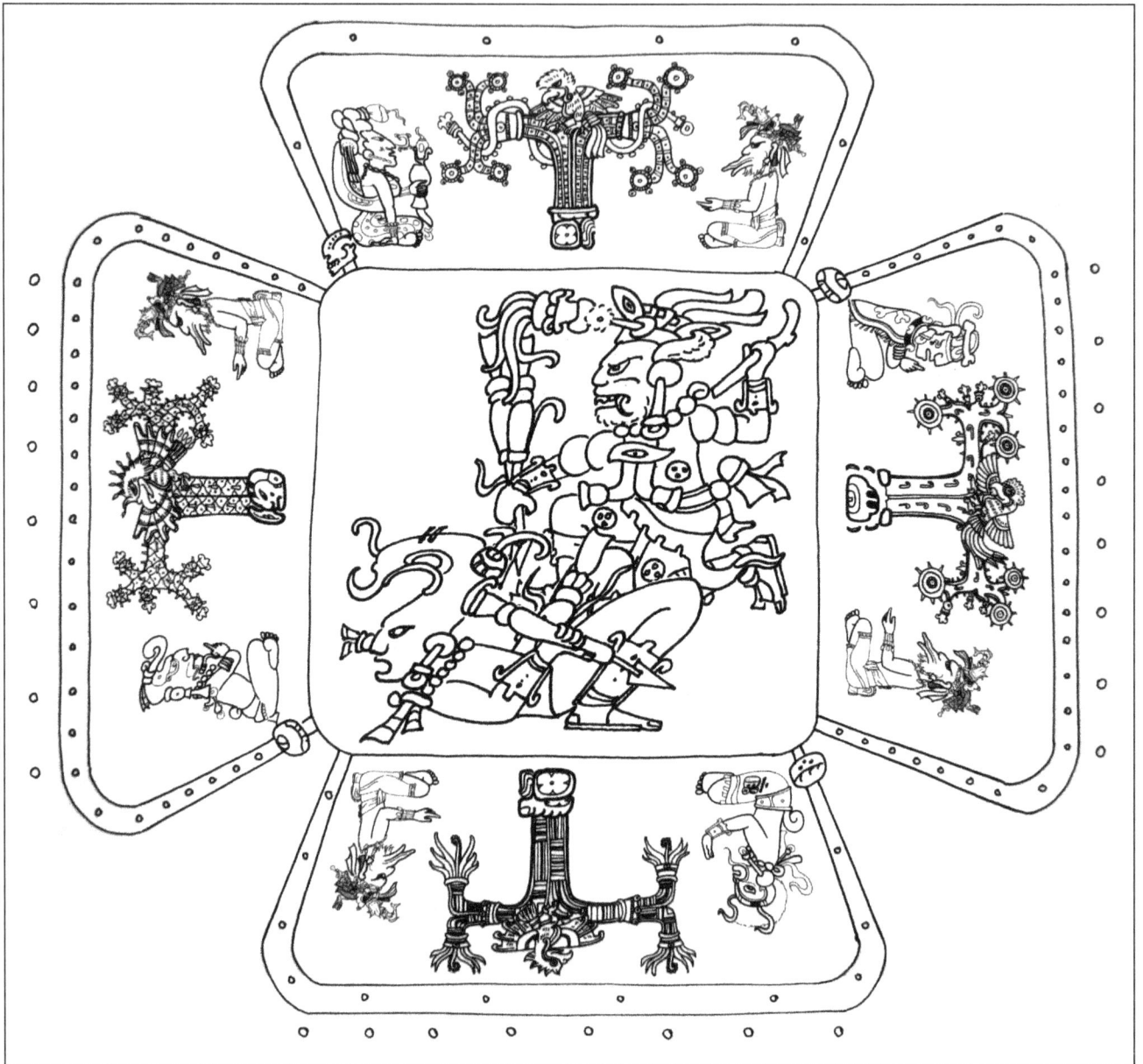

Figure 40c: Graphic representation of the Dresden Codex Venus Table, Pages 48, according to the interpretation of K'AL presented in this manuscript

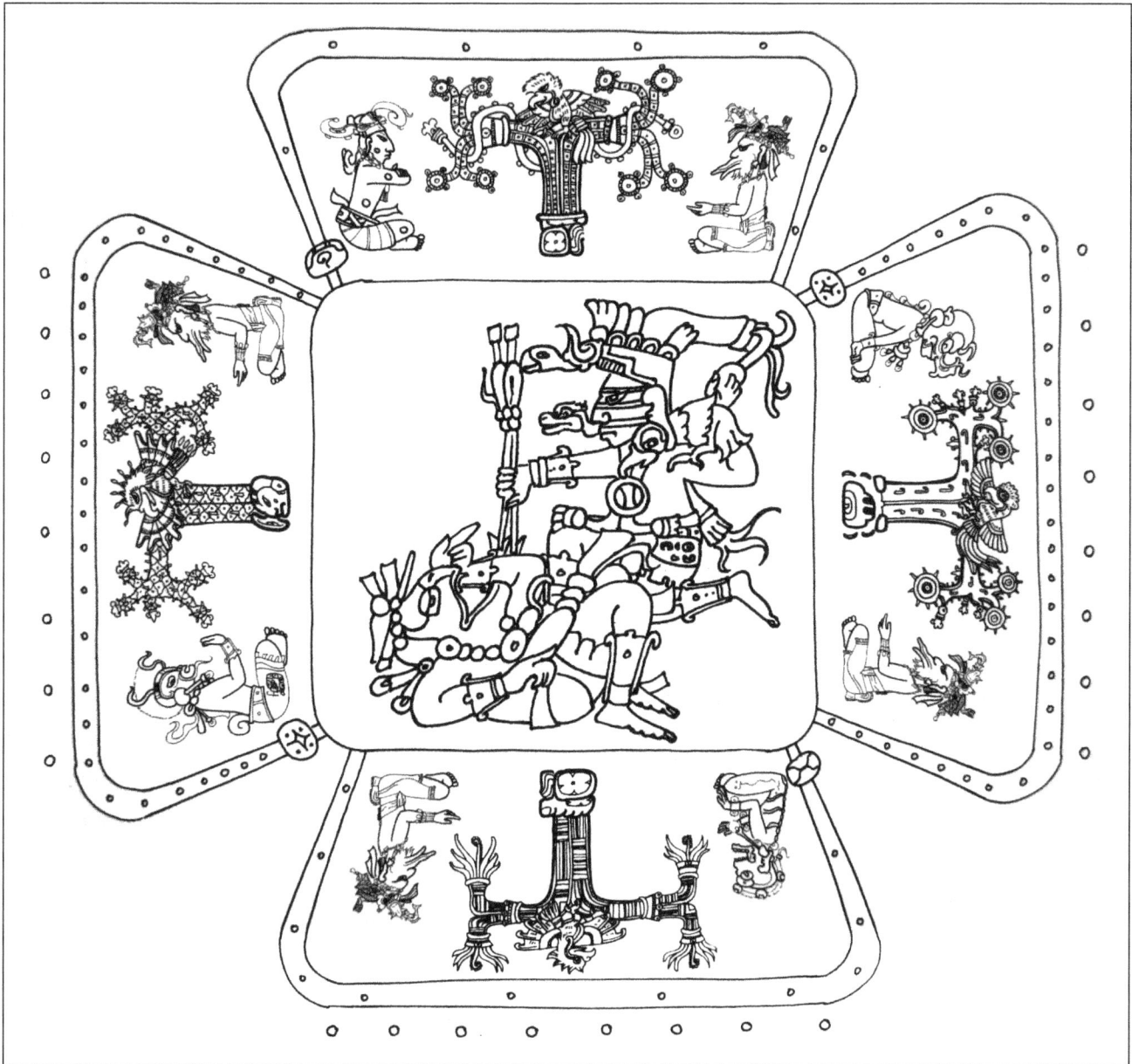

Figure 40d: Graphic representation of the Dresden Codex Venus Table, Pages 49,
according to the interpretation of K'AL presented in this manuscript

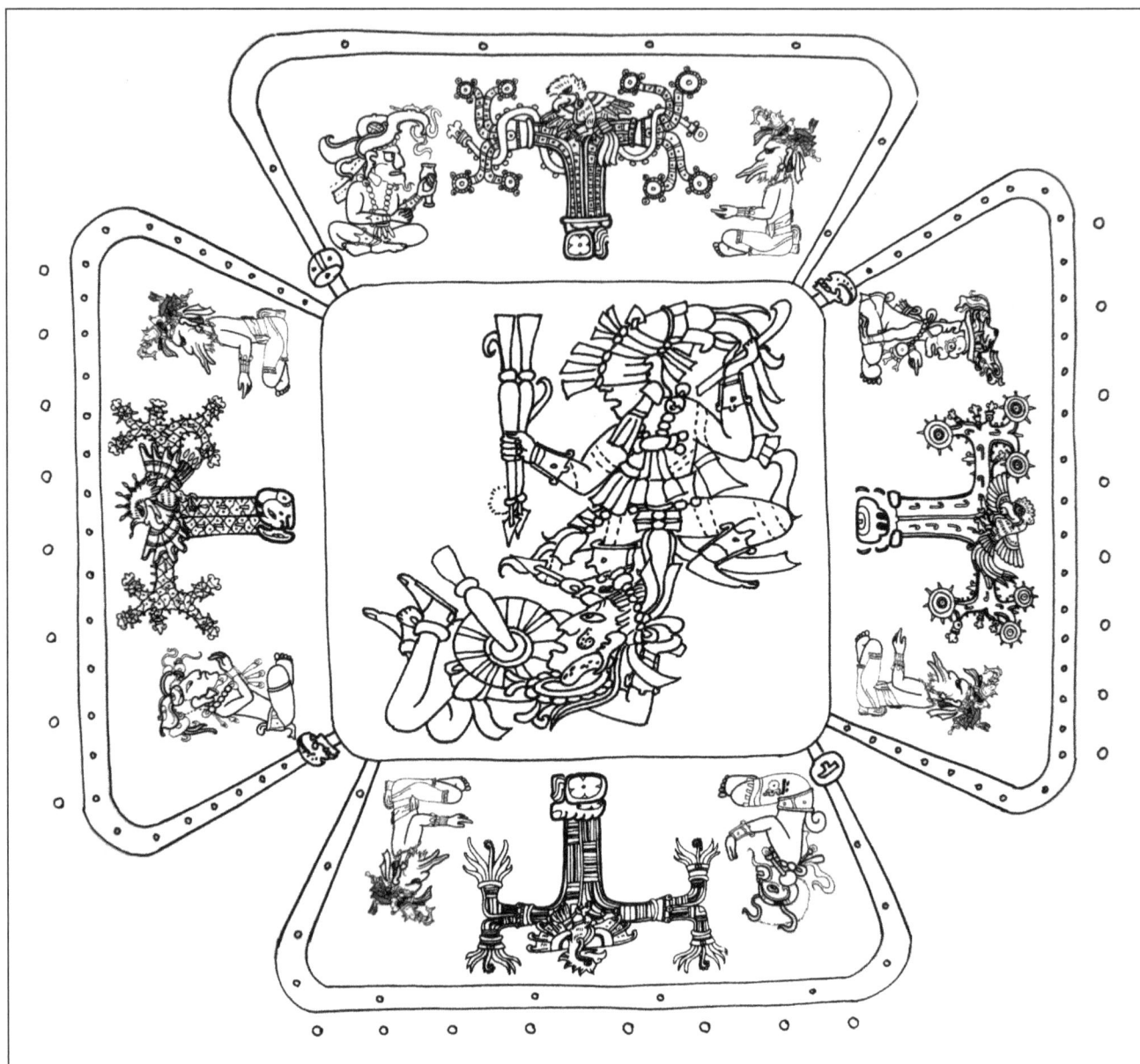

Figure 40e: Graphic representation of the Dresden Codex Venus Table, Pages 50,
according to the interpretation of K'AL presented in this manuscript

Bibliography

ALDANA, G. (2001). *Oracular Science: Uncertainty in the History of Maya Astronomy*. Ph.D. Dissertation, History of Science Department. Cambridge, MA: Harvard University.

ALDANA, G. (2004). El Trabajo del Alma de Janahb Pakal: la cuenta de 819 días y la politica de Kan Balam. In *IV Mesa Redonda de Palenque* (pp. 283–309). México, D.F.: Instituto Nactional de Antropologia e Historia.

ALDANA, G. (2002). Solar Stelae and a Venus Window: science and royal personality at Classic Maya Copan. *Archaeoastronomy Supplement to the Journal for the History of Astronomy, 27* (JHA, xxxiii (2002)), S30-S50.

ALDANA, G. (2006). Lunar Alliances: shedding light on conflicting Classic Maya theories of hegemony. In T. Bostwick and B. Bates (Eds.) *Viewing the Sky Through Past and Present Cultures: Selected Papers from the Oxford VII International Conference on Archaeoastronomy* (pp. X). Phoenix, AZ: Pueblo Grande Museum.

ALDANA, G. (2007). *The Apotheosis of Janaab' Pakal: Science, History, and Religion at Classic Maya Palenque*. Boulder, CO: University Press of Colorado.

ALDANA, G. (2007). Maya Astronomy as an Oracular Science: Thoughts on the Philosophical Under-pinnings of Indigenous Sciences. Paper presented at the Society of American Archaeology, 72nd Annual Meeting, April 27.

ALDANA, G. (2009). Aveni Honoured. Book review of *Skywatching in the ancient world: new perspectives in cultural astronomy*. *Journal for the history of astronomy, v. 40, no. 1*, 109-113.

ALDANA, G. (2009). K'AL as Ritual Enclosing at Copan and in the Dresden Codex Venus Pages: Revealing an 80-Year Detour in the Study of Ancient Mayan Astronomy. Paper presented at the CSULA Conference on Mesoamerica: Continuity and Change in Mesoamerican History from the Pre-Classic to the Colonial Era, May 15-16.

ALDANA, G. (2010). "The Maya Calendar Correlation Problem." In *Calendars and Years II...*

AVENI, A.F. (2001). *Skywatchers: A Revised and Updated Version of Skywatchers of Ancient Mexico*. Austin, TX: University of Texas Press.

BARRERA VÁSQUEZ, A. (1995). *Diccionario Maya* (3ª ed.). México D.F.: Editorial Porrúa.

BRICKER, H. & BRICKER, V. (2007). When was the Dresden Codex Efficaceous? In C. Ruggles & G. Urton (eds.) *Skywatching in the Ancient World: New Perspectives in Cultural Astronomy Studies in Honor of Anthony F. Aveni*, Mesoamerican Worlds Series (pp. 95-120). Austin, TX: University of Texas Press, 2007.

CALNEK, E. (2007). Kirchhoff's Correlations and the Third Part of the Codex Borbonicus. In C. Ruggles & G. Urton (eds.) *Skywatching in the Ancient World: New Perspectives in Cultural Astronomy Studies in Honor of Anthony F. Aveni*, Mesoamerican Worlds Series (pp. 83-94). Austin, TX: University of Texas Press.

COE, M. (1992). *Breaking the Maya Code*. London: Thames and Hudson.

DIAZ, G. & RODGERS, A. (1993). *The Codex Borgia: a full-color restoration of the ancient Mexican manuscript*. New York: Dover.

FASH, W. (1991) *Scribes, Warriors, and Kings: the city of Copan and the ancient Maya*. London: Thames and Hudson.

FASH, W. & FASH B. (1996). Building a world-view: visual communication in Classic Maya Architecture. *RES: Anthropology and Aesthetics, No. 29/30*, 127-147.

FÖRSTEMANN, E. (1891). Explanation of the Maya Manuscript of the Royal Library of Dresden. N. Thomas (translator). *Bureau of Ethnology, 2022*, 81-124.

FÖRSTEMANN, E. (1894). Page 24 of the Dresden Maya Manuscript. *Zur Entzifferung der Mayahand-schriften, IV, Dresden*, 431-443.

GILLESPIE, S. and JOYCE, R. (1998). "Deity relationships in Mesoamerican cosmologies: The case of the Maya God L." *Ancient Mesoamerica* 9: 278-296.

HOUSTON, S., ROBERTSON, J., & STUART, D. (2000). The Language of Classic Maya Inscriptions. *Current Anthropology, 41, 3,* X-Y.

HRUBY, Z. & CHILD, M. (2006) "Chontal Linguistic Influence in Ancient Maya Writing: intransitive positional verbal affixation." In *The Linguistics of Maya Writing.* (pp. 13-26) Edited by Soren Wichmann. University of Utah Press, Salt Lake City.

HULL, K. (200). *An Abbreviated Dictionary of Ch'orti' Maya.* Final Report for the Foundation for the Advancement of Mesoamerican Studies, Inc. (FAMSI), grant #03031.

JUSTESON, J. & TAVAREZ D. (2007). The Correlation beteen the Colonial Northern Zapotec and Gregorian Calendars. In C. Ruggles & G. Urton (eds.) *Skywatching in the Ancient World: New Perspectives in Cultural Astronomy Studies in Honor of Anthony F. Aveni,* Mesoamerican Worlds Series (pp. 17-81). Austin, TX: University of Texas Press.

KAUFMAN, T. (2003). *A Preliminary Mayan Etymological Dictionary.*

KETTUNEN, H. & HELMKE, C. (2009). *Introduction to Maya Hieroglyphs, 14th European Maya Conference Workshop Handbook.* Cracow: Wayeb and Jagiellonian University.

LACADENA, A. (2006). Passive Voice in Classic Mayan Texts: CV-*h*-C-*aj* and –*n*-*aj* Constructions. In S. Wichmann (ed.) *Linguistics of Maya Writing* (pp. 165-194). Salt Lake City, UT: University of Utah Press.

LOUNSBURY, F. (1978). Maya Numeration, Computation, and Calendrical Astronomy. In C.C. Gillespie (ed.) *Dictionary of Scientific Biography, Volume 15,* (pp. 759-818). New York: Charles Scribner's Sons.

LOUNSBURY, F. (1992). Derivation of the Mayan-to-Julian Calendar Correlation from the Dresden Codex Venus Chronology. In A.F. Aveni (ed.) *The Sky in Mayan Literature,* (pp. 184-206). New York: Oxford University Press.

LOUNSBURY, F. (1992). A Solution for the Number 1.5.5.0 of the Mayan Venus Table. In A.F. Aveni (ed.) *The Sky in Mayan Literature,* (pp. 207-215). New York: Oxford University Press.

MATHEWS, P. (2001). Notes on the Inscriptions on the Back of Dos Pilas Stela 8. In *Decipherment of Ancient Maya Writing,* (pp. 394-415). University of Oklahoma Press.

MATHEWS, P. & BÍRO, P. (2008). *Maya Hieroglyph Dictionary.* Retreived from: http://research.famsi.org/mdp/mdp_index.php

MILLER, M.E. (1988). The meaning and function of the Main Acropolis, Copán. In E.H. Boone and G.R. Willey (eds.) *The Southeast Classic Maya zone: A symposium at Dumbarton Oaks, 6th and 7th October 1984,* (pp. 149–94). Washington, D.C.: Dumbarton Oaks Research Library and Collection.

NEWSOME, E. (2001). *Trees of Paradise and Pillars of the World: the serial stela cycle of "18-Rabbit-God K," King of Copan.* Austin, TX: University of Texas Press.

PAXTON, M. (2001). *The Cosmos of the Yucatec Maya: Cycles and Steps from the Madrid Codex.* Albuquerque, NM: University of New Mexico Press.

POWELL, C. (1997). *A New View on Maya Astronomy.* Masters of Arts Thesis. Austin, TX: University of Texas.

ROBERTSON, J., HOUSTON, S. & STUART, D. (2004). Tense and Aspect in Maya Hieroglyphic Script. In S. Wichmann (ed.) *Linguistics of Maya Writing,* (pp. 259-289). Salt Lake City, UT: University of Utah Press.

SATTERTHWAITE, L. (1947). *Concepts and structures of Maya Calendric Arithmetic.* Ph.D. Dissertation. Philadelphia: University of Pennsylvania.

SCHELE, L. (1999). *Notebook for the XXIIIrd Maya Hieroglyphic Forum at Texas.* Austin, TX: Department of Art and Art History, University of Texas.

SCHELE, L. & FREIDEL, D. (1990). *A Forest of Kings: The Untold Story of the Ancient Maya.* New York: William Morrow.

SCHELE, L. & GRUBE, N. (1997). *Notebook for the XXIst Maya Hieroglyphic Workshop.* Austin, TX: Department of Art and Art History, University of Texas.

SCHELE, L. GRUBE, N., & FAHSEN, F. (1992). The Lunar Series in Classic Maya Inscriptions: New Observations and Interpretations. *Texas Notes on Precolumbian Art, Writing, and Culture,* 29.

SCHELE, L. & MILLER, J. (1983). The Mirror, the Rabbit, and the Bundle: "accession" expressions from the Classic Maya Inscriptions. *Studies in Pre-Columbian Art and Archaeology, 25,* 1-99.

SELER, E. (1904). Venus Period in the Picture Writings of the Borgian Codex Group. In *Mexican and Central American Antiquities, Calendar Systems, and History.* Translated from the German under the supervision of Charles P. Bowditch. *Smithsonian Institution Bureau of Ethnology, Bulletin 28,* 355-391.

STUART, D. (1995). *A Study of Maya Inscriptions.* Ph.D. dissertation, Department of Anthropology. Nashville: Vanderbilt University.

STUART, D. (1996). Kings of Stone: a consideration of stelae in ancient Maya ritual and representation. *RES, 29/30,* 148-171.

STUART, D. (1996). Hieroglyphs and History at Copan. *Workbook for the Harvard Field School.* Cambridge, MA: Harvard University.

STUART, D. (2005). *The Inscriptions from Temple XIX at Palenque.* San Francisco: Pre-Columbian Art Research Institute.

STUART, D. (2006). *Sourcebook for the 30th Maya Meetings*. Austin, TX: The Mesoamerica Center, Department of Art and Art History, University of Texas.

STUART, D. (2007). *Sourcebook for the XXXI Maya Meetings*. Austin, TX: The Mesoamerica Center, Department of Art and Art History, University of Texas.

STUART, D. (2008). *Copan Archaeology and History: New Finds and New Research. Sourcebook for the 32nd Maya Meetings*. Austin, TX: The Mesoamerica Center, Department of Art and Art History, University of Texas.

TATE, C. (1992). *Yaxchilan: the design of a Maya ceremonial city*. Austin, TX: University of Texas Press.

TAUBE, K. & BADE, B. (1991). An Appearance of Xiuhtecuhtli in the Dresden Venus Pages. *Research Reports on Ancient Maya Writing 35*. Washington D.C.: Center for Maya Research, 13-24.

TEEPLE, J. (1931). Maya Astronomy. In *Contributions to American Archaeology, Volume 1, Nos. 1 to 4*. Washington D.C.: Carnegie Institution.

THOMPSON, J.E.S. (1971 [1950]). *Maya Hieroglyphic Writing: An Introduction*. Norman: University of Oklahoma Press.

THOMPSON, J.E.S. (1972). *A Commentary on the Dresden Codex*. Philadelphia: Memoirs of the American Philosophical Society, vol. 93.

VELASQUEZ, E. (2006). The Maya Flood Myth and the Decapitation of the Cosmic Caiman. *PARI Journal, Volume VI, No. 4*, 1-10.

WALD, R.F. (2004). The Languages of the Dresden Codex: Legacy of the Classic Maya. In S. Wichmann (ed.) *Linguistics of Maya Writing*, (pp. 27-60). Salt Lake City, UT: University of Utah Press.

WATANABE, J.M. (1983) "In the World of the Sun: A Cognitive Model of Mayan Cosmology." In *Man* n.s. 18 (4), 710-728.

WHITTAKER, G. (1986). The Mexican Names of Three Venus Gods in the Dresden Codex. *Mexicon 8, 3*, 56-60.

WICHMANN, S. (2004). The Linguistic Epigraphy of Maya Writing: Recent Advances and Questions for Future Research. In S. Wichmann (ed.) *Linguistics of Maya Writing*, (pp. 1-12). Salt Lake City, UT: University of Utah Press.

WISDOM, C. (1950). *Chorti Dictionary*. Transcribed and transliterated by Brian Stross. Austin, TX: Department of Anthropology, University of Texas.